50 Drills for Debating and Public Speaking

The big book of activities & exercises for debate & public speaking training

www.debate.training

Philip & Katherine Johnston

The thinking behind this book

Hundreds of drills were considered for this compilation; those that made this Top 50 had to be:

- Readily graspable. So that coaches don't lose time & momentum having to clarify how a new drill works. If a drill couldn't be thoroughly explained in a single page, it's likely to be too complicated to use with students.

- Challenging. Our experience has been that students are most switched on when the task is daunting, the demands high, and the time limit unreasonable. The drills in this book will stretch students, often beyond anything they're likely to encounter in an actual debate or speech.

- Repurposable for different skill levels. Not just so coaches can use the same drill with different groups, but so they can accommodate multiple skill levels within the one group, from novices through to the most experienced of debaters.

- Targeted. So that coaches know what each drill is *for*. Every drill in the book is cross-referenced by the skill it addresses so you can find the drills you need quickly.

- Involving the whole group. Either through mass participation, rapid turnover in the spotlight, or tasking the audience with quests of their own. These drills are designed to make your sessions too busy for anyone to be disengaged.

Drill Finder

Look up the skills you
want to develop...

🗨 Examples & Evidence

Being able to produce the facts, statistics, case studies, quotes and historical data that supports your case, and destroys your opponents'.

🗨 Impromptu Speaking

Being able to speak after short or no preparation.

The relevant drills are
listed alongside

Drill Finder

To focus on this...   ...these drills are recommended

🗨 Brevity

Being able to present complex ideas in as few words as necessary...but no fewer.

01	5 Word Debates
02	Chaotic Segues
03	Condensing Smoke
07	Duels to Zero
14	Groundhog Impromptus
21	Lightning Debates
24	One-Breath Debates
28	Poisoned Words
44	Time Lords

🗨 Engagement

These drills pit students against each other, either in teams, or as individuals.

01	5 Word Debates
02	Chaotic Segues
04	Conjurer of Examples
06	Duels
07	Duels to Zero
12	Freeze Frame Debates
17	Hostile Press Conferences
18	I Couldn't Disagree More
20	The Lifeboat
21	Lightning Debates
22	The Moderator
23	Monotrack Adjudicators
24	One-Breath Debates
25	The Panel
31	Quotemaster
32	Reason Tennis
37	Soothsaying
41	Statmaster
43	Three Columns
44	Time Lords
45	Time Out Debates
46	Tongue Twisters
47	Topic Bingo
50	You vs the World

🗨 Examples & Evidence

Being able to produce the facts, statistics, case studies, quotes and historical data that supports your case, and destroys your opponents'.

04	Conjurer of Examples
08	Evaluating the Source
30	Prompt Sheet Speeches
31	Quotemaster
38	Speed Bulletpointing
40	Stat Forger
41	Statmaster
43	Three Columns
45	Time Out Debates
50	You vs the World

🗨 Impromptu Speaking

Being able to speak after short or no preparation time—because for most of the engagement that happens in debate, that's how long you'll have.

01	5 Word Debates
02	Chaotic Segues
06	Duels
09	Expert Press Conferences
11	Four Corners
13	Grand Introductions
14	Groundhog Impromptus
17	Hostile Press Conferences
18	I Couldn't Disagree More
19	Join the Dots
20	The Lifeboat
21	Lightning Debates
22	The Moderator
25	The Panel
27	Pass the Parcel
28	Poisoned Words
29	Preassembled Debates
30	Prompt Sheet Speeches
32	Reason Tennis
34	Rescuing Boring
36	Someone Else's Notes
38	Speed Bulletpointing
39	Starter Thoughts
42	The Story Chair
43	Three Columns
44	Time Lords

Drill Finder

To focus on this...	...these drills are recommended
Inner clock Developing an awareness of how to pace your delivery and content so that an 8 minute speech is not all burned out after 6 minutes... or half done when time's up.	**06** | Duels **07** | Duels to Zero **42** | The Story Chair **44** | Time Lords
Multitasking So you can simultaneously read a note from a teammate, take in an opponent's speech, and still come up with the scorching rebuttal you need for your opener.	**02** | Chaotic Segues **06** | Duels **10** | Extreme Multitasking **22** | The Moderator **28** | Poisoned Words **50** | You vs the World
Note Taking Capturing everything that matters, and nothing that doesn't—so you have all the relevant points, themes, examples and evidence from the debate so far.	**03** | Condensing Smoke **26** | Parts of the Speech **06** | Duels **30** | Prompt Sheet Speeches **07** | Duels to Zero **38** | Speed Bulletpointing **10** | Extreme Multitasking **45** | Time Out Debates **12** | Freeze Frame Debates **50** | You vs the World **16** | Guided Tour Debates **22** | The Moderator

Drill Finder

To focus on this...	...these drills are recommended	

🗨 Novice Development
Drills that work well even if the student has no debate experience whatsoever. (And still work well even if they do, in case your group is mixed)

04	Conjurer of Examples	27	Pass the Parcel
06	Duels	28	Poisoned Words
09	Expert Press Conferences	31	Quotemaster
11	Four Corners	32	Reason Tennis
12	Freeze Frame Debates	34	Rescuing Boring
13	Grand Introductions	35	Side Effects
14	Groundhog Impromptus	39	Starter Thoughts
16	Guided Tour Debates	40	Stat Forger
17	Hostile Press Conferences	41	Statmaster
18	I Couldn't Disagree More	42	The Story Chair
19	Join the Dots	44	Time Lords
20	The Lifeboat	45	Time Out Debates
23	Monotrack Adjudicators	46	Tongue Twisters
25	The Panel	48	UnSpeeches
26	Parts of the Speech	49	Worthy Plans, Evil Plans

🗨 Opposition prep
Anticipating and preparing refutations for whatever your opposition is likely to come up with.

05	Debating Against Yourself	20	The Lifeboat
06	Duels	25	The Panel
07	Duels to Zero	37	Soothsaying
08	Evaluating the Source	45	Time Out Debates
12	Freeze Frame Debates	50	You vs the World

🗨 Rebuttal
The art of dismantling your opponent's case, one point at a time.

01	5 Word Debates	21	Lightning Debates
03	Condensing Smoke	22	The Moderator
04	Conjurer of Examples	24	One-Breath Debates
05	Debating Against Yourself	33	Rebuilding the Debate
06	Duels	35	Side Effects
07	Duels to Zero	37	Soothsaying
08	Evaluating the Source	43	Three Columns
17	Hostile Press Conferences	45	Time Out Debates
18	I Couldn't Disagree More	50	You vs the World

🗨 Reflecting
Being able to summarize what another speaker has just said; not only accurately, but more cogently and memorably than it was originally put.

03	Condensing Smoke
05	Debating Against Yourself
06	Duels
22	The Moderator
45	Time Out Debates
50	You vs the World

Drill Finder

To focus on this...	...these drills are recommended	

☙ Speechcraft

So that you're compelling to listen to, and give your arguments the best possible chance of not only being *heard*, but *remembered*.

01	5 Word Debates	31	Quotemaster
02	Chaotic Segues	34	Rescuing Boring
03	Condensing Smoke	36	Someone Else's Notes
04	Conjurer of Examples	40	Stat Forger
13	Grand Introductions	41	Statmaster
14	Groundhog Impromptus	42	The Story Chair
24	One-Breath Debates	44	Time Lords
28	Poisoned Words	46	Tongue Twisters
29	Preassembled Debates	48	UnSpeeches
30	Prompt Sheet Speeches		

☙ Structure and Roles

The mechanics of how debates actually work, and understanding the roles of each speaker.

05	Debating Against Yourself	26	Parts of the Speech
12	Freeze Frame Debates	29	Preassembled Debates
15	Guess the Topic	33	Rebuilding the Debate
16	Guided Tour Debates	36	Someone Else's Notes
21	Lightning Debates	37	Soothsaying
22	The Moderator	43	Three Columns
23	Monotrack Adjudicators	45	Time Out Debates

☙ Teambuilding

Icebreakers and changeups to keep your sessions lively, unpredictable and engaging.

01	5 Word Debates	28	Poisoned Words
02	Chaotic Segues	30	Prompt Sheet Speeches
04	Conjurer of Examples	31	Quotemaster
05	Debating Against Yourself	32	Reason Tennis
06	Duels	34	Rescuing Boring
07	Duels to Zero	35	Side Effects
09	Expert Press Conferences	36	Someone Else's Notes
10	Extreme Multitasking	39	Starter Thoughts
11	Four Corners	40	Stat Forger
13	Grand Introductions	41	Statmaster
14	Groundhog Impromptus	42	The Story Chair
17	Hostile Press Conferences	43	Three Columns
19	Join the Dots	44	Time Lords
20	The Lifeboat	46	Tongue Twisters
21	Lightning Debates	48	UnSpeeches
24	One-Breath Debates	49	Worthy Plans, Evil Plans
25	The Panel	50	You vs the World
27	Pass the Parcel		

Drill Finder

To focus on this...	...these drills are recommended	

💬 Triaging

Figuring out of the many things you *could* target, what you *should* target.

01	5 Word Debates		16	Guided Tour Debates
03	Condensing Smoke		21	Lightning Debates
05	Debating Against Yourself		22	The Moderator
06	Duels		24	One-Breath Debates
07	Duels to Zero		30	Prompt Sheet Speeches
10	Extreme Multitasking		38	Speed Bulletpointing
12	Freeze Frame Debates		45	Time Out Debates

💬 Working co-operatively

Drills that have students working together in groups.

12	Freeze Frame Debates		35	Side Effects
15	Guess the Topic		37	Soothsaying
16	Guided Tour Debates		41	Statmaster
26	Parts of the Speech		45	Time Out Debates
29	Preassembled Debates		47	Topic Bingo
31	Quotemaster		50	You vs the World
33	Rebuilding the Debate			

💬 More online

For more resources and publications, visit the official debate.training website.

www.debate.training

The drills

With notes for busy debate coaches

💬 5 Word Debates

TWO SPEAKERS GOING HEAD TO HEAD, but each speaker is only allowed a maximum of 5 words when it's their turn. Can they be concise—and precise—enough to successfully debate the motion when every statement they make is slogan-length?

01

Good for: Brevity • Engagement • Impromptu Speaking • Rebuttal • Speechcraft • Teambuilding • Triaging

💬 How this works

Choose your combatants, give them a topic:

That cars should be banned

They'll be taking turns speaking, similar to **REASON TENNIS ▶ 32**, except that each time they speak they're limited to just 5 words.

💬 Speaker roles for this

With only 5 words to play with, there isn't room to accommodate rebuttal and argument advancement in the same statement, so the roles of each speaker need to be constrained:

Affirmative's job each time is to propose a different argument in defense of the motion.

Negative's job is simply to rebut whatever argument they've just heard.

Since they can only respond, negative's task is a little tougher here, and is generally better suited to the more experienced of the two debaters.

💬 An example

A 5-word debate consisting of 4 rounds on the topic "that cars should be banned" might sound like this:

====ROUND 1==========

Aff: Cars cause significant pollution
Neg: *Electric* cars don't cause pollution

====ROUND 2==========

Aff: Car accidents cost countless lives
Neg: Drinking, speeding; not cars' fault

====ROUND 3==========

Aff: Roads use too much space
Neg: Roads make high density possible

====ROUND 4==========

Aff: Not walking makes us fat
Neg: Not driving keeps us isolated

There's no need for an adjudication. Once the two speakers have finished, load up another topic, find two more speakers, and run another debate.

💬 If it proves too hard...

Two things you can do to make life easier for speakers:

1) You can run a debate using the same format, but with a more generous word limit.

2) You can give speakers time to prepare: again, negative has the harder job here, because they need to anticipate affirmative arguments and come up with rebuttals for each.

💬 *Countdown* debate

If you have two speakers who are ready for an even tougher challenge, run a debate with exactly 10 rounds, and a word limit that starts at 10, and then drops by one for each subsequent round. So in round 2 there would be a 9 word limit, round 3 an 8 word limit...and so on, until the final round, when each side only gets to say one, very carefully chosen word. Keep the transcripts—they make entertaining reading :)

💬 Chaotic Segues

02

IMPROMPTU SPEAKING can be daunting enough…but what if the assigned topic were to change every 20 seconds, *while the student is still talking?* Can the speaker think quickly enough—and produce bump-free segues—so that all the crazy shifts forced on them plausibly belong in the same speech?

Good for: Brevity · Engagement · Impromptu Speaking · Multitasking · Speechcraft · Teambuilding

💬 How this works

The student is given a topic, say:

Things you shouldn't have for breakfast

and must immediately start talking:

"OK, so Oktoberfest fans might disagree, but most physicians will tell you that *beer* for breakfast is not the best way to get the day underway…"

DING !!!

It's the 20 second mark, which means the moderator calls out a brand new—and entirely unrelated topic:

New York

Uh oh. That's not what the speech was just talking about…the student's job though is to continue on without missing a beat:

"…of course, it's not as though there's a *law* against beer for breakfast, but it turns out there could have been. Several years ago in New York, there was a push to outlaw drinking entirely before 8pm; hard to see how it would be enforced though."

Absolute rubbish, of course—there was no such proposal—but the student's job is to keep going, not present fact-checked journalism. In any case, 20 seconds are up, so:

***DING!!! ***

Circus Animals

And so they push on:

"One law that New York *did* implement though was a ban on live animal performances in circuses, which Sanderson Brothers Circus infamously dodged by featuring a clown act with *dead* animals…"

And so on. In two exhausting minutes, they will have had to weave six completely unrelated topics into their impromptu. By comparison, traditional single-topic impromptus should seem easy thereafter…which is the whole point.

💬 How this ends

One option is to have each student at the podium for a set time; their job is to keep going—and keep up—until the final bell rings, at which point their patchwork speech is over.

A more confronting variation is for the student to be allowed to keep going until they hesitate for the very first time. If you go the hesitate-and-you're-out option, one point scored for every topic completed turns this drill into a competition…just how far will your best students get?

💬 Topic stockpiles

This drill burns through topics *fast*—you'll need a large and varied pile to hand.

When you're creating that pile in the first place though, it will be much easier for the speaker if each prompt is not too specific; for example, **"bad weather"** is much easier to work into just about any speech than **"impact of free trade agreements on sugar cane prices"**

(then again, you may not necessarily *want* to make things easier for the speaker ☺ Mwuhahaha…)

💬 Condensing Smoke

03

THE HARDEST POINTS TO REBUT are not those that are *well* made. It's *unclear* points that can be so tricky—engaging them is like wrestling smoke. This drill is all about taking something badly phrased, ill-considered and rambling, and condensing it into a clearly explained idea. (So you can smash it later)

Good for: Note Taking · Rebuttal · Reflecting · Speechcraft · Triaging

💬 How this works

The most challenging aspect of this drill is coming up with the source material. What you're looking for is speeches that have lots of words, but are complete train wrecks otherwise...but where to look?

You have three options, in ascending order of fun.

The first option is to find the speeches online. There are tens of thousands of videos of debates/interviews with politicians/answers at town-hall type meetings with statements or entire speeches that make no sense. Trawling through them to find what you need is time consuming, but the results are worth the wait.

The second option is to write such speeches yourself, or—if you're confident enough—to improvise woolly speeches on the day. Go nuts, enjoy yourself :)

The third option is to have students produce the speeches. *Who here*, you can ask, *thinks they can make a point badly and at length, packed with thoughts that go nowhere in particular, and examples that don't really match what you're talking about?* Challenge accepted, is what you'll hear from some of the students. Brace yourself.

💬 The audience's role

Those listening need to rephrase what they've just heard so that it sounds clear and well thought out, even though it was nothing of the sort.

So you might be starting with something thoroughly flubby like this:

> "The problem with the UN and other countries like that is that wars and conflict and genocide cause more problems than they solve, such as malnutrition in countries where food is scarce and so people starve which is why we see so many ads for charities that have to feed people in Africa which is where some of these wars start in the first place, which is irony."

Which your student might turn into:

> Starvation is a hidden cost of war; just look to Africa.

Yes, you can almost hear the opposing team saying, *that's totally what I meant.*

I have no idea if that is what they meant (who knows...I mean seriously, did you *read* that?), but this condensed retelling is something that can be understood by all.

And because it's so clear, now it's rebuttable.

💬 Not straw man

This might all sound like a manifestation of the Straw Man fallacy, but you're not actually misrepresenting anything here. *The aim should be to present their speech in it's best light*; to extract whatever points might be hidden in there, and present them so clearly that village idiots trapped in a sack could understand them.

The fact that you were able to deftly make such sense of what was otherwise an unholy mess will not be lost on the audience, or the adjudicator...but being able to do it takes practice. Comes in handy more often than you might think :)

Conjurer of Examples

04

D EBATE STUDENTS KNOW THAT compelling examples are not just persuasive, but *adhesive*: they stick in the minds of adjudicators and audiences long after the speaker has finished. Coming up with such examples on the spot is not so easy though...this drill gives students practice in doing exactly that.

Good for: Engagement · Examples & Evidence · Novice Development · Rebuttal · Speechcraft · Teambuilding

How this works

This drill is focused very much on students coming up with *lots* of examples for a given prompt; the logic is that students are much more likely to stumble on a killer example in a debate if their candidate list is long.

You'll need a timer, and an extensive stockpile of prompts; once a prompt has been written on the board, students would have 90 seconds to come up with as many examples as they can.

When time is up

At the end of the 90 seconds, ask the students how many examples they were able to come up with. Start with the student who came up with the most; record on the board any examples on their list that you felt met the prompt's criteria.

Once you're done, rather than collecting entire lists from each of the remaining students, the only hands you want in the air now are students with responses that *aren't* on the list you already have up.

As each new example is written up, you'll see hands steadily go down, until you've collected everything the room had.

Voting and scoring

With all examples now on the board, students need to vote for the two they thought were the most compelling. Scoring then works as follows:

- Any student whose response contained the most-voted-for example scores 3 points.

- If a student's list contained the *second*-most-voted-for example, they score 1 point.

- A student whose list both contained the top response, and the runner up would score 6 points.

- The student with the longest list of valid examples would score a bonus 10 points.

Example prompts

The prompts should be accessible enough that all students should readily be able to come up with several examples:

Laws that save lives

Why it would be hard to be poor

Things that governments have to spend money on

be sure too to include some that are not so serious:

Things babies should not be allowed to play with

or infinitely open-ended

Things you would not be expecting to find in your fridge

Be ready to be amazed by what your students come up with.

The tougher version...

Instead of having time to think and write down examples, put a student at the podium, and fire your prompt at them: they have to come up with three valid examples on the spot.

The catch? They have to list all three within 10 seconds, otherwise they're out, and someone else takes their place...how many rounds can they survive?

💬 Debating against Yourself

I T'S A SIMPLE ENOUGH IDEA: one debater, speaking for both sides of the same debate. At its heart though it's a powerful way for students to learn to make their own cases more resistant to attack—how well can they identify, exploit, and then ultimately defend weaknesses in their own arguments? They're about to find out...

05

Good for: Opposition Prep · Rebuttal · Reflecting · Structure & Roles · Teambuilding · Triaging

💬 How this works

There's fun to be had here with the absurdity of what's about to unfold—the whole thing is very much like the Monty Python sketch where Monty "Bomber" Harris wrestles himself.

Set up two desks out the front, as if a regular debate were about to unfold, have the student sit at one of them.

Reveal the topic and introduce the first speaker for the Affirmative. After the applause, they'll defend the proposition just as a first Affirmative might.

Once the speech is finished though, instead of the speaker sitting back where they started, they sit at the other desk, waiting their turn as 1st Speaker of the Negative. Introduce them as that now; once they get to the podium they'll quickly summarize the key points from their first speech...

...and then destroy it as completely as they're able, before laying out an alternative.

💬 It can end there

If you're looking to give several students an opportunity in a short space of time, limiting each student to speaking once *in favor*, and then immediately once *against* the motion can suffice.

However that really is the lite version. If you've got the time, much better is to give students the experience of speaking in *every position for an entire debate*—there is really no better way for them to emerge with a solid understanding as to what each speaker is for than to have had to become each in turn.

One compromise if time is an issue is to simply tighten the speaking times; the student would still be playing every role in the debate, but might only be speaking for 45 seconds for each.

💬 Note disadvantage

The single most difficult challenge in this exercise is not the dual role, but the fact that the speaker will be unable to take notes during each speech. Keeping track of which

arguments have been made, which have been rebutted and what those rebuttals have been can quickly get out of hand, even though the same student was responsible for coming up with all of it.

One solution is for the speaker to have others on their team who don't actually have a speaking role themselves, but can take notes. The speaker would have an opportunity to confer with these note-takers briefly before each speech, and can use whatever palm cards or notes they come up with.

💬 Beginner version

This exercise works well even with students who are not ready for full debates—simply make a contestable statement, and then have the student give two reasons in support, then immediately switch and give two against. An embryonic version of opposition prep, easy enough even for novices.

💬 Duels

06

IT LOOKS LIKE CHAOS: pairs of students, toe-to-toe, all doing battle simultaneously in a series of zero-preparation, short one-on-one debates. Here's why you want it in your bag of tricks: there's no audience for duels, which makes these debates *safe* for nervous or novice students.

Good for: Just about everything, but a great drill particularly for notice debaters

💬 Setting up

Have the students pair up, so that they're comfortable with whoever they're up against first, but let them know that they'll be rotating through different partners as the activity progresses.

Arrange the pairs into two lines, and give everyone the topic: all those lined up on the left are affirmative, those on the right will oppose.

💬 Keeping it moving

To keep the duels short, and rotations to new partners frequent, limit speaking time to 60 seconds for affirmative, 90 seconds for negative, with a final 30 seconds right-of-reply to affirmative, so that they also have an opportunity to rebut.

💬 Cutting through the din

With so many debates happening at the same time, the room will sound more like a stock exchange trading floor than a classroom—you'll need a referee's whistle to indicate the end of each speech, or you'll probably not be heard at all.

Because those involved in the duel really are standing toe-to-toe, there should be no problem hearing each other...however, the background racket protects first time debaters from being heard by anybody else. This truly is safety in numbers.

💬 How the flow works

1: First, give everyone the topic. Then tell the affirmatives that they have 60 seconds, and that their time starts in 3 - 2 - 1... *Whistleblast*

Off they go. Half the room is now arguing affirmative for the same topic, while negative listens and plans their response; it will be mayhem.

2: 60 seconds later, give another whistleblast to return the room to silence. Tell the negative speakers that they have 90 seconds, that they should use the first 30 seconds to rebut what they've just heard, and that their time starts in 3 - 2 - 1... *Whistleblast*

Now the negative has launched, the room is a din once again.

3: 90 seconds later, one more whistleblast to return the room to silence again. Tell the affirmative speakers that they have a final 30 seconds to rebut what the negative had to say. Their time starts in 3 - 2 - 1... *Whistleblast*

4: Final whistleblast to return the room to order and end the debate. There is no result, no adjudication, just a thank you to sparring partners, and then rotation to a new partner.

Lather, rinse and repeat for as many rounds as are needed.

💬 Involving parents

If your workshop includes younger students, duels are a great way for parents or caregivers to be engaged at pickup time. Have adults line up opposite their own child, give the topic, explain the rules, blow your whistle, and let the arguing commence.

Duels to Zero

07

TWO DEBATERS TAKE TURNS SPEAKING, but each subsequent speech is 5 seconds shorter than the speech immediately before it. Can the debaters zero in on what's important as the ever-shrinking time limit makes the irrelevant too costly to include?

Good for: Brevity · Engagement · Inner Clock · Notetaking · Opposition Prep · Rebuttal · Teambuilding · Triaging

How this works

Choose your duelers, call them to the podium, give them a topic. The affirmative opens by speaking for 60 seconds in support of the resolution; negative then replies in 55 seconds.

Because the speakers are alternating, the affirmative is then next to speak again; they have to fit that reply into 50 seconds. When negative responds to that, they'll talk for 45 seconds...and so on, until the final negative speech, which is just 5 seconds long.

Triaging to time

As the time limits shrink, the debaters will be forced to tackle the most pressing points first, otherwise they might not get to them at all. The focus of this exercise then really becomes identifying just what those most pressing points are.

If you only had 5 seconds to land a telling blow, you can ask them, *what would you say?*

For the negative, that's not just a hypothetical—at the very end of the

debate, 5 seconds is exactly what they'll have. They're going to have to be very smart about how they use that time.

Cut from the bottom

When the speaking times are getting crazy short, one of the best ways for students to figure out what to focus on is to create a list of what *doesn't* warrant coverage.

The aim here is to stop students from rebutting simply by picking low hanging fruit—if you've only got 5 seconds, you don't have time to target Vulnerable-But-Peripheral points.

The takeaway for students? *What* you target ultimately matters more than *how hard* you hit your target or *how many* targets you hit. As any military commander will confirm, blowing up something irrelevant not only wastes ammunition, it leaves the critical targets standing safely.

Give time to think

While the speeches themselves are subject to strict time limits, it's worth giving students thinking time between

speeches—that final 5 second speech is going to be much easier to give if the student had 30 seconds to get their head around it first.

Add it up. It's not fair.

Add up the speaking times, and you'll realize that affirmative gets 210 seconds of speaking time in the whole debate (60+50+40+30+20+10), while negative only gets 180 seconds (55+45+35+25+15+5). The message you can give your debaters? Yes, it's not fair. Deal with it. (Or you can simply assign negative to the more experienced speaker)

Try it in reverse

Start with 5 seconds for affirmative's first speech, then add 5 seconds for every speech thereafter, up to a limit of 60 seconds for the final negative speech. Again, the time constraints force the debaters to think tactically about what to include, and what not to—these reverse versions are great for laying out up front what they key issues will be.

Evaluating the Source

RESEARCHING IS DIFFICULT because finding information is easy—from a single search term, a student can list tens of millions of potential sources. Most of that will be dreck though; this drill helps students develop their critical skills so they can tell what's trustworthy, what's questionable, and what's just plain crazy.

Good for: Examples & Evidence • Opposition Prep • Rebuttal

Finding the sources

To prepare for this, you'll need a range of different sources that you've harvested from the web, representing all degrees of the credibility spectrum.

So there will be articles from Foreign Affairs magazine side-by-side with a rant from a survivalist website; surveys on smoking and health sponsored by Big Tobacco together with similar studies (with presumably very different conclusions) from the New England Journal of Medicine; opinion pieces from conservative think tanks, vs those from their liberal counterparts.

The aim is for each to illustrate a different principle of source credibility, either in the observance, or the breach.

Scoring them

The students' job is to assign each source a rating for trustworthiness and unassailability:

- A **10** means the source is so credible that the information could withstand any challenge. So, for example, a foremost international expert on bees explaining what impact pesticides can have on pollination.

- **0** would mean that the source is so compromised, biased or untrustworthy that the information is better left unsaid. So just because the Weekly World News has a piece explaining how aliens are helping keep the price of oil artificially high, then that doesn't mean you should be quoting it in your debate about renewable energy.

Most sources will fall somewhere between, but make sure you've got some genuine 0's and 10's in the mix, so that there's a clear point of reference.

Questions to ask

The list below is by no means exhaustive, but will have students well on their way to knowing whether a source is unimpeachable, may be subject to attack, or unquotable:

- Is the author a stakeholder who stands to lose or gain if whatever they're proposing/cautioning against is adopted/prevented?

- Is the author a genuine expert on whatever subject they're being quoted on?

- Has this author been cited as an expert by other leading experts in the field?

- How recent is the information?

- If the claim is scientific, is it peer reviewed?

- Who is the publisher? A university press? A Ministry of Communication in a dictatorship? An advertising agency?

- Does the source cite sources, and if so, are they also credible?

- Does the information contain qualifiers, passive voice or weasel words that leave room for the statement to mean something else entirely?

The aim of the drill is not so much to answer these questions, but for students to know they have to ask them in the first place.

Expert Press Conferences

09

ONE STUDENT IS AT THE PODIUM, playing the role of a randomly assigned expert or public figure, while the rest of the group peppers him/her with questions. Can the student handle the press conference with credibility and confidence, even though they have to make up every answer on the spot?

Good for: Impromptu Speaking • Novice Development • Teambuilding

Creating the scenario

Tell the student at the podium who they're supposed to be, and why they're suddenly in the spotlight—for example:

- A scientist trying to downplay a toxic leak from a nuclear reactor.
- A rock star explaining why she's boycotting France for her next tour.
- An airline executive defending the decision for their airline to charge infants a "nuisance traveler" levy.
- A politician seeking to be re-elected, despite double digit unemployment, and a soaring crime rate.

If you're stuck, trawl the news, find a controversy, modify as needed.

Start the questions

To set the tone, give the first couple of questions yourself, but you want to throw it open to the floor as soon as you can—students drive this one.

Vetting questions

If a question is inappropriate, unhelpful or rehashing previously answered material, interrupt and explain to the questioner why you won't be expecting an answer for that, and tell them they're welcome to raise their hand again once they've come up with a better one.

Keep it snappy...

This exercise is as much for those asking the questions as it is for the person at the podium—the aim is for high turnover with short, clear, credible answers, rather than speeches. If they're monologuing, interrupt and move things along.

...or make it a stretch

Alternatively, if you require a minimum speaking time for each response, Press Conferences are also a great way to gently stretch students who otherwise struggle to make it to speech time limits. The logic is that if the student can fill their speaking time when they have no idea what they're talking about, then a regular debate—with its prepared material on a researched subject—will be easy by comparison.

Scaling to suit

You can control how tough this exercise is by being smart about the type of expert you're expecting the student to be. So, for example, for an experienced debater with strong general knowledge, you might try this:

> **"Please welcome to the podium Dr. Lisa Feldman, who has just written a book pushing for Brazil to be included as the 6th permanent member of the UN Security Council"**

Alternatively, for a student who has never debated before, and is nervous about the idea of speaking in front of anybody, disarm the moment with something lighter:

> **"And now, Mr. Dennis Sedgewick, here to tell us about his record-breaking collection of snails..."**

Not every question in Press Conferences has to have the students fixing global warming, or engineering peace in the Middle East ☺

Extreme Multitasking

DEBATERS WAITING TO SPEAK have a lot of plates to keep spinning: they need to *take notes,* come up with *rebuttals, triage* incoming arguments, mentally *rehearse* how they might begin their speech...there's a lot going on, and there's no pause button. This drill is all about learning to cope with the chaos.

10

Good for: Multitasking · Notetaking · Teambuilding · Triaging

How this works

This drill works well as an everybody-at-once exercise. Make sure the students have something to take notes with, and have them listen to a speech while they capture every key point.

That's one of their jobs; if they were free to concentrate on just that, there would be no problem.

But there's more. While they're listening to the speaker and taking notes, they also need to be completing a sheet that's filled with basic arithmetic problems. Adding columns of numbers, working out how many legs 12 chickens, 25 donkeys and 2 three-legged dogs have between then...that sort of thing. Easy, but demanding of their attention.

By the time the speech is finished, the arithmetic sheet needs to be done, and their notes need to be complete.

Identifying downtime

For students to survive this drill, they need to know when it's safe to temporarily *stop* taking notes—for example, if a speaker is giving an extended illustration of a point that the note-taker has already captured. Since they wouldn't have been taking further notes during this anyway, it's safe enough to squeeze in a few quick arithmetic questions; as soon as the speaker switches to a fresh point, the math sheet would be put on hold, while the new note is taken.

Other task options

Instead of a math sheet, students might have to come up with a *list of names that start with the letter M,* or *animals that shouldn't be pets.* It doesn't really matter, as long as it periodically pulls their attention away from the notes they're supposed to be taking.

To mirror more closely the sort of mental juggling that happens in actual debates, then they could be tasked with coming up with points to support a given proposition, or examples to support a given point. All the while, they'd still need to be keeping an ear on what the speaker is saying, and taking notes whenever anything new/important is said.

Dialing it up...

As students cope with the 2-task multitasking, throw a third into the mix...and then a fourth.

So, for example, as well as having to record key points in the speech, they might have to rank them, from "Strong" through to "Questionable"; they might have to come up with rebuttals for each, or they might have to come up with a point of their own that isn't mentioned in the speech.

The busier you can make the student—and the more "multi" the multitask challenges—the better they'll be able to cope with the plate-spinning reality of standard debates.

Complete overload...

Have a student who is coping with it all? You might need to turn this drill up to "max"...give them a crossword puzzle to complete, notes to take, *and* a speech on a different topic to prepare...and if that's still not enough, have them take notes for two *simultaneous* speeches :)

Four Corners

AN ICE-BREAKING DRILL for students new to debating: the students hear a statement, and then stand in one of four corners of the room, depending on the extent to which they agree/disagree with what they've just heard. Once in position, they can be called upon to explain *why* they've chosen the corner they have...

11

Good for: Impromptu Speaking • Novice Development • Teambuilding

Introduce the corners

Take the students on a tour of the four corners of the room: one for each of:

- Strongly Agree
- Gently Agree
- Strongly Disagree
- Gently Disagree

Make sure the two "Strongly" corners are diagonally opposite each other; that way one side of the room will be *for* the proposition, the other will be *against*.

Choosing the topic

Something commonplace enough that everyone is likely to have an opinion without requiring specialist knowledge. So:

"Winter is better than summer"

is a better option than:

"Social security payments should be indexed to movements in average weekly earnings rather than CPI"

Starting comfortable

This exercise is all about sneaking up on public speaking. So when you begin, look for short answers, with the student addressing you directly as the moderator. It won't feel like public speaking, so much as simply answering a question, as they would have countless times at school.

The next step though is to ask the student to present exactly the same defense a second time, but this time in front of an audience. Of *course* you can do it, is the message. You just *did*.

Stretching the time

By now they've justified a position in front of an audience; the next step is to add a minimum time to any statements they make. It's one thing to give a one sentence answer to justify their position; it's another entirely to have to talk without stopping for 30 seconds.

Adding basic clash

Ramping up this drill doesn't have to stop with minimum speaking times—you can also throw in some primordial rebutting. As soon as a student has finished defending their position, invite someone with an opposing viewpoint to challenge with a sentence that begins "Yes, but surely...". Once they're coping with that, then you can invite right of reply, and we're just a few formalities away from an actual debate.

Swapping sides

OK, so the students can advocate for their own position...can they also advocate equally effectively for an opposing viewpoint? Tell all the students to stand on the opposite side of the room, and be ready to defend their new position.

Advanced Students

Four Corners is not just for beginners—it's also a tidy way to test advanced students' mastery of particular ethical or policy issues. Put the proposition, let them stand where the will—or actively place them—then have them defend where they find themselves.

Freeze Frame Debates

12

IT'S A TACTIC USED by sports coaches the world over: watch a replay of a game with the players present, and hit pause periodically to talk about what's just happened...and what perhaps should have happened instead. Like sports, debates happen *fast*—it's easier to point things out when you can freeze the action.

Good for: Engagement • Notetaking • Novice Development • Opposition Prep • Structure & Roles • Triaging • Working Co-operatively

The video version

To run this version of the drill, you'll need a video of a debate—preferably involving the debaters who will be hearing the post-match analysis. Load it up, make sure everyone can see.

As feedback occurs to you—positive, negative, or simply suggestions—don't just note it down. Pause the video the instant it occurs to you, and talk about it while it's running hot.

If the assembled students aren't sure what you're referring to, rewind, watch the moment again, this time while their radars are tuned to the issue—it will take on a whole new significance. It's one thing to tell a student that they overuse "um when they speak; it's another entirely to confront them with the evidence.

Student commentators

If you're running the video version, another essential perspective is the student's—throw them the remote control, and allow them to pause and comment at any time during their own speech. You'll hear all sorts of things that might not have emerged otherwise:

> "..yeah...here I couldn't remember the word 'negotiation', got myself into a tangle while I flummoxed around for an alternative."

> "...I freaked out here because time was almost up, and I still hadn't got to my second point, so everything from here on in was five times as fast as it should have been."

> "Just stopping here...wow...I didn't realize that I look down at my palm cards so much..."

Use their own feedback as a springboard for conversation—and the basis for a pledge that whatever they mess up in future, it won't be *that*.

The live version

An alternative way to run the same drill is to forget about videos, and work with an actual, right-there, live debate.

Again, you have the power to pause at any time to give feedback—it's a much more potent option than simply talking about it

afterwards, because students have the opportunity to fix things while they're actually speaking. So if you pause to tell a student that so far, they're speaking too quietly, they can redeem themselves in what remains of their speech once you hit "resume" again.

Taking a Mulligan

A powerful way to ensure that students are actually absorbing feedback is to also video the student taking a second swing at whatever they got wrong the first time.

So our student who was caught saying "um" all the time will be recording 60 seconds without saying "um" once. Similarly, the student who wasted time rebutting the wrong points will video the rebuttal he/she wishes was given.

Of course, the students don't get second chances like this in actual debates—but if they regularly run this drill, they'll be less likely to need such a second chance in the first place.

💬 Grand Introductions

13

A PART FROM BEING a novice-friendly impromptu speaking drill, being able to make introductions is one of the most common of all public speaking scenarios. As ever, there's a twist here: in this drill, the students will be introducing people—and things—that normally would never be introduced by anyone...

Good for: Impromptu Speaking · Novice Development · Speechcraft · Teambuilding

💬 Modeling this

This is a drill that's going to be easier for you to demonstrate than explain; those watching will very quickly understand what's required.

The core idea is that you'll be making an introduction, as though you were welcoming someone—or something—to the podium.

Start by telling the room what you've been tasked with introducing—the subject doesn't have to be a person—and then brainstorm three features of the introductee.

So, for example, if you had to introduce a **sheep**, they might tell you:

- Gives wool
- Groups are flocks
- Not the brightest animals

From that, you've got everything you need to make the welcome:

"Best known for hanging out in flocks, and a straightforward, no-nonsense anti-intellectual approach to life, these are the animals that make our woolly winterwear possible. Could you please welcome: *sheep*."

All three brainstormed elements were present in the introduction, but joined seamlessly.

If the topic instead had been "mountains", the brainstorm might have produced:

- They're very high
- Good for skiing on
- Mountain goats live on them

Which might produce the following introduction.

"A home for goats, a skiers' paradise, and so tall that only superman can jump over them... could you bang your hands together and make some noise as you give it up for MOUNTAINS!!!!"

By now the students should get the idea, and you can throw the third intro to a volunteer.

💬 Possible topics

Pretty much anything that the students would be familiar enough with to be able to make a handful of points:

- Famous people (how might they introduce *Beethoven*, for example?)
- Kitchen appliances (toaster? Fridge?)
- Professions (plumber? geriatric nurse? zookeeper?)
- Shapes (triangle? octagon? fractal?)
- Plants (Cactus? Venus Fly Trap? Rosebush? Bamboo?)

You get the idea. Just about anything can be introduced.

💬 Intro...then Q&A(!)

A fun way to extend this is for the introduction to be followed by a student then assuming the role of whatever was being introduced, and then taking the podium for a question-and-answer session, similar to the game **EXPERT PRESS CONFERENCES ▶ 09.**

This is as challenging for the audience as it is for the person at the podium—what on earth would you ask an octagon? Or a toaster?

Groundhog Impromptus

I T'S THE SAME TOPIC OVER AND OVER, while the student struggles to keep coming up with a constant stream of fresh 10 second speeches. As soon as they hesitate, repeat an idea, fill with fluff, or go off-topic, they're out...how many rounds can they survive?

14

Good for: Brevity • Impromptu Speaking • Novice Development • Speechcraft • Teambuilding

How this works

Call a student to the podium, and give them a topic to speak on—something open-ended such as:

Dogs

or

Bad weather

so that there are immediately countless ways they could tackle it.

After a countdown of 3-2-1, they then have to give an impromptu speech for 10 seconds on that topic. That's obviously very short, so they have to get straight to the point—it's not enough time to finish a speech, but it is enough for you to be able to tell if they were going somewhere with it.

Once time is up, there's another countdown, then they have to immediately give another 10 second speech...but on exactly the same topic. They cannot repeat any idea from their first speech, hesitate, pack it with fluff, or drift from the topic.

If they're successful, then they need to give a third speech, which is not allowed to reuse any ideas from the first two...and so on.

An example

So, taking "Dogs" for a moment, the student might open with this:

"Dogs are traditionally known as man's best friend; fair enough, as they're easy going, loyal and protective in a way that, say, a puma would not be..."

DING! Time's up. New countdown starts: 3-2-1...off they go again...

"Dogs might be offended to know that the species is often used as an insult: you *dog*, I'm *dog-tired*, food not fit for a *dog*..."

DING! Again, that's time. No chance for respite, new countdown is already underway: 3-2-1...

"Dog rhymes with *frog*, and *log*, and *cog*, and *hog*; interestingly half of these "og" words are also animals, like "dog" itself. Linguists might wonder if this is more than coincidence..."

OK, so that's spurious in the extreme...but it's a new take, sticks to the topic and there were no hesita-

tions. That's a green light from this judge. On we go 3-2-1:

"Dogs are friendly and excellent companions, it's no wonder they're such popular pets..."

BZZZZT! Way too close to the very first speech, that's it, the student is out.

So is this next students, straight away, as they talk about "tables"

"I like tables very much, indeed, yes sir-ee, tables tables tables, like them lots, yes I do, not sure why I like them so much, I mean who knows really."

No hesitations in there, but no content or central idea either—that's all filler. Similarly, even if the content is excellent, if there *are* hesitations, they're gone too.

⚡ Can anyone get to 10?

It's the four minute mile of Groundhog Impromptus...can any student complete 10 in a row?

Guess the Topic

IT'S NOT SO MUCH public speaking as detective work. Teams are drip fed fragments of an actual debate—statistics, pithy quotes, citations, snippets of rebuttals and case outlines—from which they are then racing to work out what the topic must have been.

15

Good for: Structure & Roles · Working Co-operatively

How this works

This drill is set up as a contest: the aim is to use the given debate fragments to become the first team to correctly guess what the topic had been.

The teams take turns; before they make their guess, they're allowed to confer for 30 seconds. The team's captain then states their guess.

If they were correct, then they score a point, a new topic is selected, and the game moves on to a fresh round. If they weren't correct, then the next team has 30 seconds to confer, and then make a guess of their own...and so it continues until someone nails it.

Drip feeding clues

Prior to a team taking their turn, a clue to the topic is revealed to everyone present. These clues are a fragment from an actual debate on the topic: a select few words from a point or rebuttal, a piece of supporting evidence, perhaps even an excerpt from an adjudication. With each freshly revealed clue, teams

should be able to gradually piece together what the original topic should have been.

So, for example, a clue might be:

> "The animals involved spend around 11 months in every year traveling in cramped conditions."

The team might confer, and decide that the topic might have something to do with eating meat, and guess the following:

> "That we should all become vegetarians"

Good guess, but not right. A few clues later and a sharp student spots the word "performances" in a given snippet, prompting the correct guess:

> "That circuses should be banned from using animals"

That team scores the points, winning the round; a new hidden topic is selected, and the game moves on.

Choosing snippets

The fragments can be as long or short, specific or general, clear or cryptic as you wish. It's usually best

if early round snippets are shorter, more general and more cryptic, with each subsequent fragment becoming more detailed, specific, and directly suggestive of the topic.

Variations

To help ensure that guessing doesn't drag on, every team is allowed to ask one wildcard question. Allowable wildcard questions are:

> "Is the word [insert word here] in the topic?"

> "What is the [n]th word in the topic?"

> "What are the first letters of each word in the topic?"

Once a team has asked their wildcard question, they've spent their opportunity to do so again until the topic has been revealed. (The moderator can always issue fresh wildcard question permits if they feel the round is dragging on too long).

💬 Guided Tour Debates

SIMILAR TO FREEZE FRAME DEBATES ▶12, a video and a pause button allows the coach to discuss what's happening, but this time the focus is simply on helping new debaters understand how debating works. Speaker's roles, signposted elements, timing considerations...all laid bare with running commentary.

16

Good for: Note Taking • Novice Development • Structure & Roles • Triaging

💬 How this works

First of all, you need to set up a debate, preferably between teams that already know what they're doing, using whatever debating rules your students are likely to have to work with in competition. As is the case throughout this book, those rules may differ from the examples given below, but you can easily substitute with whatever you need.

Whatever rules you are working under, similar to FREEZE FRAME DEBATES ▶ 12, once the debate is underway, you'll be able to pause the debate at any time; *unlike* Freeze Frame Debates though, you won't be giving feedback to individual speakers. Instead, you'll be providing commentary for those watching, as you make clear exactly what's happening in each phase of what they're seeing.

So as soon as the debate starts:

"Chairperson, ladies and gentlemen"

PAUSE. Now you discuss: do debates *have* to start with this? If not, what are the other options? Are

you free, for instance, to cold open with a quote that will be referred to in every speech on your team? If you are starting by acknowledging those present, who exactly do you acknowledge?

RESUME

"The topic of tonight's debate is that the voting age should be lowered to 15. We on the affirmative define "voting age" to mean..."

PAUSE.

Again, you explain—what's going on here? Why is the first speaker starting with a *definition?* What's a definition anyway? And once they're done with that, just what are they likely to do *next?*

Let's see if they do.

RESUME

And so on. It might take 15 minutes to work through a 2 minute speech in this way; so be it. But at the end of that time, the audience will know what every part of that speech had been *for*—which gives them a better chance of being able to construct such a speech for themselves.

💬 What to comment on

Any element a student must include in their own debates, from case outlines to rebuttals, supporting evidence to signposting, salutations to closing zingers. When you're running a Guided tour debate, the assumption should be that anything you don't stop and comment on will be something students then won't know how to do.

💬 Learning. To. Play.

This whole process is very similar to how you probably learned many board and card games as a kid: the very first game is not competitive, but a stop-start affair as your parents explain every step. *Here's how we choose who goes first; let's take a look at your cards now and see what you might do; ok, let's see what the next player might play in response...and so on.* The guided tour stops players from feeling lost—which makes it much more likely they'll enjoy the game.

Hostile Press Conferences

17

S IMILAR TO EXPERT PRESS CONFERENCE ▶ 09, a student is at the podium, ready to field questions, but this time they're up there to defend a given position from a room full of journalists who have assembled for one reason only: to grill them with a severity that would make Socrates blanch.

Good for: Engagement · Impromptu Speaking · Novice Development · Rebuttal · Teambuilding

Setting the parameters

First introduce the student and the position they're supposed to be defending. It's not a debate, so there's nothing wrong with outlining a position that has several parts—it means more for the journalists to ask questions about:

"Our guest's latest book controversially suggests that anybody who is jailed should be jailed for life.

It also maintains though that we should only be jailing a tenth of the people we currently do.

Here to take your questions on this is the author, Jessica Jenkins."

Or it could be something quite stark:

"Parents need classes in parenting. So says Arpad Kellerman; he's here now to answer your questions."

Whatever the topic, ask the first question to set the tone, then throw it open to the floor...and let the hunt begin.

Every so often...

Give a topic that will strike everyone as being all but indefensible:

"Our next speaker believes that Olympic athletes should be able to pump themselves full of whatever drugs they need to maximize their performance."

Seems like a tough ask for the student at the podium, but as any seasoned political journalist will tell you, the pressure here is actually on the questioners—can they come up with interrogation that actually does lay bare the flaws in the proposition? Or is there merely indignation, but no knockout blow?

Vetting questions

As for EXPERT PRESS CONFERENCES ▶ 09, If a question is inappropriate, unhelpful or rehashing previously answered material, explain to the questioner why you won't be expecting an answer for that, and tell them they're welcome to raise their hand again once they've come up with something better.

Look for followups

At any point in time, there's likely to be a lot of hands in the air, but that doesn't have to mean that questions are pot luck. You can filter what should be next by asking if any of the questions relate directly to the answer that was just given.

If you feel it's a thread that still has life, then these are the questions you want next; if the thread has been flagging though, you can tell those students to find another issue, and pick someone else for a fresh angle.

It's not personal

This is indeed a hostile press conference, but only in the sense that the questions are all very much focused on finding cracks in the student's argument—none of the hostility can be directed to the student personally.

This activity is a perfect vehicle for reminding students that while debate can be both intense and merciless on underprepared ideas, the attacks should always be focused on then content, not the person delivering it. (Not just because personal attacks are *mean*; but because they're *weak*.)

💬 I Couldn't Disagree More...

I T'S ZERO-PREP-TIME REBUTTAL, in an informal and simplified format. The moderator makes a statement, and then a student is chosen to respond; they have to commence that response with "I couldn't disagree more...", together with all the reasons, evidence and logic they are able to summon in, well, no time at all.

18

Good for: Engagement • Impromptu Speaking • Novice Development • Rebuttal

💬 Calibrating the trigger

The moderator has tremendous power over just how difficult this challenge is, depending on what trigger statement they choose, which makes this game suitable for a huge range of experience levels. For apprehensive or first-time debaters, topics can be self-evidently attackable:

> "The driving age should be lowered to 5 years old"

At the other end of the continuum, topics could require the most cynical of devil's advocacy, or nuanced attention to detail in the statement's wording:

> "Wherever possible, wars should be avoided"

Preschoolers on our freeways is one thing, but what does a student do with this second topic? Are we about to hear a defense of *realpolitik?* Or an examination of the unclarified "avoided *by whom?*", as they follow with a spirited condemnation of soldiers who go AWOL rather than put themselves in harm's way? The game—and the sophistication of the rebuttal it demands—is very much a function of the topic put forward, and will scale to just about any group you're ever likely to work with.

💬 It's all in the *why*

Part of the point of this exercise is for students to come away understanding that simply asserting rejection of an idea is the easy part, and that debating demands much more. Take for example:

> "That all old people should be killed on their 75th birthday"

Here, the response "I couldn't disagree more!" will tumble out quickly; what probably won't tumble out so quickly is then a clear articulation as to *why* the proposal should be rejected. Simply protesting *it's just wrong*, is not enough—the key question, which needs to be developed with clarity and rigor—is *"why"*.

💬 The group variation

If you're working with students who need the rebuttal development, but aren't ready to be put on the spot for impromptu responses just yet, another way to run the same drill is to have students working in small teams. They'd have the opportunity to confer briefly when they hear the topic, and then would be offering "we couldn't disagree more" as part of a joint response.

💬 Alternative aff cases

This drill also works as preparation for debate formats that require case extensions, such as British Parliamentary debating—you just need to modify the antecedent statement slightly:

> "I largely agree, however..."

The rest of that statement is devoted then both to pointing out flaws in the current proposal, and putting forward an alternative model that largely supports the same ends, but is more efficient/ more likely to be successful/has fewer downsides etc.

A useful reminder to students that not all opposition has to be based on *polar* opposition.

💬 Join the Dots

19

THE SPEAKER IS GIVEN two completely unrelated events, 60 seconds to think, and then must demonstrate how the first event could cause the second. How could *planting a tree* cause *2 million deaths?* Or A *law banning the sale of soft drinks* trigger an *arms race?* This is the post hoc fallacy, in reverse, run riot...enjoy.

Good for: Impromptu Speaking • Novice Development • Teambuilding

💬 Tree planting example

So how could a student show that **planting a tree** might cause **2 million deaths?** Their speech might run something like this:

> A tree is planted; years later a car loses control on a bend and slams into it; inside the car was a diplomat on her way to averting a civil war; her replacement proves not nearly so effective; war breaks out and rages for a decade; 2 million people lose their lives.

or perhaps

> A tree is planted. It was *supposed* to be a *billion* trees, as part of a UN project to create a carbon sink to offset the deforestation of the Amazon, but they couldn't get the funding, so a single symbolic tree was planted instead. One symbolic tree was never going to stop climate change though; decades later storms that may have been ameliorated by the carbon sink ravage South East Asia, killing an estimated 2 million people.

Neither is likely to withstand scrutiny; it's not the point. The student's job is to think quickly, come up with *something* that joins the dots (there's no time for research here...)

💬 Soft drinks arms race?

Again, from one of the examples at the top of the page—how could a **law banning the sale of soft drinks** trigger **an arms race?** The student might come up with this:

> A law is passed banning the sale of soft drinks; a leading multinational manufacturer of soft drinks then faces a choice: bankruptcy or a change of direction. They repurpose their facilities to manufacture hard-to-detect plastic firearms. The plastic weapons prove to be more reliable and cheaper to manufacture than traditional arms, driving up demand, with what happy shareholders and alarmed police chiefs alike characterize as an "arms race" for the new weapons.

💬 Have groups do battle

Another fun way to run this drill is have groups brainstorm their way to a solution...or, for bonus points, as many different solutions as they can, in (say) 20 minutes. Present, hold a vote on the best solution (groups can't vote for their own), declare a winner.

💬 Joining *nearby* dots

Focusing on linking *unrelated* events is a potent trigger for creative impromptus, but if instead the students had to show how two *plausibly associated* events could be linked, then the drill instead becomes a great way to work with current affairs.

So, for example:

> **How could** *regime change in Egypt* **cause the** *destabilization of the entire region?*

Or:

> **How could** *admitting India as a sixth member of the Security Council* **lead to** *improved relations between China and the US?*

The task this time is not to come up with a butterfly-flaps-its-wings tenuous chain, but to show how X could plausibly cause Y—students will really need to be across their current affairs to pull this off.

The Lifeboat

IT'S A CLASSIC SPEAKING DRILL—an overloaded lifeboat is within sight of a deserted island, but will sink unless several of the passengers are thrown overboard. Each student is assigned a profession; their speech must justify why they are essential for surviving what's ahead, and should be spared.

20

Good for: Engagement • Impromptu Speaking • Novice Development • Rebuttal

The easy version

The key to keeping this easy—particularly for inexperienced public speakers—is to create a list of professions which are all self-evidently useful to a fledgling society on a desert island. That way, the students will immediately have plenty of points to make.

There are plenty of others, but here are six examples:

- Carpenter
- Expert in fishing
- Expert in farming
- Expert in poisonous plants
- Doctor
- SAS survival instructor

Not so easy

If the students are more experienced, have them plead the case for professions whose utility in the desert-island survival community is perhaps a little less immediately clear, but definitely defensible with a little thought. Again, some examples:

- Teacher
- Architect
- Engineer
- Mathematician
- Scientist
- Counselor/psychologist
- Economist
- Police officer
- Politician

Tough

With no intended offence to the professions below...it's just that most desert island survival communities should be just fine without them. Unless they're all on a boat with each other, they'd normally be the first thrown off:

- Elvis impersonator
- Hypnotist
- Pickpocket
- Archaeologist
- Ventriloquist
- Composer
- Taxi driver
- Wedding planner

or include them all...

It's not even remotely fair, but *not fair* in this game is *fun*, because it can produce some hilarious speeches from the likes of pickpockets and Elvis impersonators as they try to justify their positions over the doctors and experts in fishing. (Heck, throw *actual* Elvis into the mix as well)

Warn the students that some speeches will be easier than others, then draw cards out of a hat... or assign the tough ones to the students who can cope.

Unleash mayhem

By far the most challenging—and funniest—version of this drill is to have students come up with the professions that go in the hat.

Here's the twist though: *let them know that if they draw the profession they created, they'll get to redraw.* The significance? They're immune from whatever they contribute :)

After a moment's thought, you'll see the evil grins on the students' faces...

Lightning Debates

A RAPID-FIRE DRILL that has a new debate launching every 2.5 minutes: 30 seconds prep time; 30 seconds speaking time for each side; 30 seconds adjudication; 30 seconds to draw the next topic out of a hat...and start the process all over again. En garde...

21

Good for: Brevity · Engagement · Impromptu · Rebuttal · Structure & Roles · Teambuilding · Triaging

Laying the groundwork

Because everything is so relentlessly quick, there's no time for organizing or gathering materials once you're underway—all the elements you need have to be in place before you start:

- A hat full of topics
- A timekeeper who will be moving the debates to the next phase every 30 seconds.
- An adjudicator who is able to give a result and a couple of reasons for their decision in just 30 seconds.
- A queue of aff speakers
- Another queue of neg speakers

Phase 1: topic

The first student in each of the aff and the neg queues move to the podium, ready to debate. While they're moving into position, the topic is read out. By the time they arrive, they'll probably have 10-15 seconds of prep time, so this drill is basically impromptu.

Phase 2: speaking

Once the 30 seconds from Phase 1 are up, the timekeeper simply says "Aff", and affirmative starts speaking.

At the 30 second mark of that affspeech, the timekeeper will say "neg". No matter where aff is up to at that moment, they must *stop* talking immediately, and neg must *start* their speech.

There's no rebuttal—there's not time and it would be too mucky to adjudicate—they're just presenting points for the negative.

Phase 3: adjudication

As soon as 30 seconds is up in the neg's speech, the timekeeper simply says "adjudicator", at which point the adjudicator will begin their overview and give the result of the debate.

After 30 seconds, the Adjudicator reads out the topic of the next debate as the current debaters leave the podium, and the next students in the queue make their way...and we're back at Phase 1.

It's absolutely as insane as it sounds, and a lot of fun.

2 uses for 30 seconds

1) Make just one point, and elaborate.

> "Cars should be banned because our road toll is too high to justify the convenience of keeping them. Every year, more people die on our roads than from all wars and acts of terrorism combined—if cars were replaced with a nationwide rail system, the road toll would plummet, simply because there would be fewer opportunities for accidents in the first place. ."

2) Make a series of short points:

> "If cars were banned, there would be no need for parking stations, a dramatic drop in air pollution in our major cities, and incentive to stop urban sprawl, an environmentally responsible shift to public transport, a road toll of zero, instead of tens of thousands, and people might get some exercise once in a while, so the nation wouldn't be quite so morbidly obese...what's not to like?"

⧉ The Moderator

I T'S A STANDARD DEBATE, but with an additional neutral speaker who stands between the teams, and whose job it is to *reflect* exactly what the previous speaker had said, and then *pose the questions* that the next speaker must therefore address. Like an adjudication, but in real time...

22

Good for: Engagement · Impromptu Speaking · Multitasking · Notetaking · Rebuttal · Reflecting · Structure & Roles · Triaging

⧉ How this works

This drill is compatible with just about any debate format, including DUELS ▶ 06. Once each speaker has finished, the Moderator needs to summarize what the previous speaker had said:

> "The opening Aff speaker has just said that cars should be banned because they're dangerous, citing the fact that 34% of all hospital injuries are related to road trauma. Sounds like their key point is that we would be *safer* without cars. What does the negative say to this?"

Now that the Moderator has highlighted road trauma as a central issue, the next speaker has to deal with it. If they don't, then the Moderator is likely to follow their speech with this:

> "Still waiting to hear negative's response to the idea that cars make our emergency departments busy. If 2nd neg doesn't target this, the point may well be conceded."

The Moderator is doing more than summarizing the debate here; they're actually *shaping* it.

⧉ Keeping them honest

The main job of the Moderator is to ensure that speakers don't get away with things they shouldn't—omissions, assertions without evidence, contradictory statements.

So if a speaker makes an unsupported assertion, then the moderator would call them out in the summary.

> "We heard from opening Affirmative that lowering the school leaving age would raise the crime rate, but we didn't hear *how*. I'm hoping 2nd Aff is able to join the dots."

That 2nd speaker is now very likely to attempt to rescue the point by providing the missing evidence link, while the 1st speaker will be less likely to make unsupported claims the next time they speak.

There's nowhere to hide when the Moderator is in the room; speakers quickly learn this, and the debates are better for it.

⧉ Not for beginners

The role of Moderator is best suited for experienced debaters, or those training to be adjudicators. If you don't have such students present, then the debate coach can fulfill the role.

⧉ Moderate, then speak

An extension of this is to require each speaker to be the Moderator immediately before their own speech. That way, they're laying bare how they see what was just said, and what they're hoping to accomplish in the speech they're about to give.

Self-aware speakers who have a reason for every sentence, and assess every possible point and rebuttal for its tactical and strategic significance? Only the best debaters can do that. It starts with drills like this.

Monotrack Adjudicators

23

ONE STUDENT SPEAKS, everyone else adjudicates. But these are no ordinary adjudicators: each has been assigned a different single technical issue—an obsession—which *all* their feedback must target. For the speaker, there is no hiding from the scrutiny of the Monotrack Adjudicators...

Good for: Engagement • Novice Development • Structure & Roles

How this works

Before the speech, assign each adjudicator a different single issue to focus on—their job is to create in-depth feedback on that one issue to the exclusion of everything else.

So, for example, one adjudicator might be told to concentrate on ensuring the speaker is **projecting their voice** well enough to be heard by all...they'll probably position themselves up the back of the room to assess this.

Another might be focusing on **fillers**, counting "ums" and other empty noises.

The next student might be assigned to check **eye contact**, while the student next to that might be assessing how dependent the speaker is on their **notes**—a related, but slightly different technical issue.

Throw in students checking **diction**, variation in **pacing**, use of **time** and use of **hand gestures** respectively, and the speech is already well on the way to being thoroughly covered from a multitude of perspectives.

Not just technical

Adjudicators can also be tasked with assessing content as well. If it's a debate, one adjudicator might focus on the **accuracy of characterizations** of what the opposing team is supposed to have said, another on the **effectiveness of rebuttal**, while another might assess the **choice** of what was rebutted in the first place.

There can be adjudicators focused on use of **humor**, strength of **metaphors**, clarity of **signposting**, presence of **clichés**, use of **statistics** and **supporting evidence**, inclusion of **fallacies**...the options are as extensive as the list of issues you wish your debaters would get right.

Relentlessly thorough

The result is that if a speaker hears from 20 of their peers, they will also have had their speech assessed for 20 different elements—it's coverage that traditional say-whatever-you-like feedback simply cannot match for either breadth, or depth.

A second swing

The sheer variety of feedback can be overwhelming for the speaker— one way to see what's sticking is to give them an opportunity to give the speech a second time once the feedback is complete.

When the monotrack adjudicators then give their feedback second time around, all they need to do is confirm which of the two speeches was better (from the point of view of their given obsession). The speaker's aim is to ensure most of those reports confirm "was better second time."

Mixing it up

Another variation is to video the speech, and then have those giving feedback watch it multiple times—but each time to be allocated a different obsession. The adjudicators will quickly discover that the same speech can seem very different, depending on which technical or content elements you're listening for.

One-Breath Debates

I**T'S ALL ABOUT MAKING EVERY WORD COUNT:** students' speeches are not limited by *time,* but by how much they can fit into a *single breath.* What will the students say when they've only got a sentence or two? What if they approached entire debates with this kind of precision?

24

Good for: Brevity · Engagement · Rebuttal · Speechcraft · Teambuilding · Triaging

How this works

This drill is a less extreme version of 5 word debates—depending on their lung capacity and breath control when they speak, they should be able to get through half a dozen sentences.

The idea is that the debate otherwise runs as normal, but before each speech, the speaker takes in a deep breath, and then must deliver everything they have to say in a single breath. As soon as they run out of breath—or are caught snatching a quick breath—they have to sit down.

Removing fluff

With only a handful of sentences to work with, there's no time for students to waste on salutations. If a student starts with

> "Chairperson, members of the audience, tonight's topic is timely, given recent events: that mining in Antarctica should be banned. We on the affirmative believe..."

then we might never actually find out what the Affirmative believes.

Similarly, empty phrases aren't going to be merely annoying padding; they actually risk leaving the student with no content at all:

> "We've heard a number of interesting points from the other team tonight, but they obviously haven't thought everything through; there are a number of flaws in their case I'd like to take a moment to point out before commencing my substantive material."

37 words, all signposting what's *about* to happen, but nothing actually *has* happened yet. There have been no points made, no rebuttal launched; the transcript itself could have been taken from any of thousands of debates.

The whole point of the drill is for students to develop a sensitivity to—and intolerance for—fluff in speeches. There's a huge difference between an 8 minute speech, and an 8 minute *content-dense, relentlessly targeted* speech; that's a big ask for students in training, so One-Breath debates has them producing a 15-30 highlights package.

Rapid turnover

One-breath speeches don't last long...which means that the debates themselves are over quickly, often too quickly to do more than skim the surface of any issue.

One solution is to allow speakers to speak several times each in the course of the debate. If they have three points to make, then each could be the focus of a separate speech; that then allows time for each point to be supported by reasons and evidence.

Keeping this drill *safe*

There are not many debating drills that are potentially dangerous, but you don't want students passing out and hurting themselves. Speakers need to be seated for this drill; you also need to be aware of any students with asthma, or other potential breathing impediments. Give them the option, but better perhaps that they adjudicate rather than participate in this drill.

The Panel

I**T'S A FORMAT THAT MAKES GREAT TV;** a proposition is discussed by a panel of diverse and clashing stakeholders, with questions contributed by viewers or a studio audience. What will your students say as they advocate for the interest they've been assigned? And can your audience come up with questions that rattle?

25

Good for: Engagement • Impromptu Speaking • Novice Development • Opposition Prep • Teambuilding

How this works

The key to this is to go beyond the usual aff/neg dichotomy, and instead find an issue that would produce a spectrum of opinions, depending on the nature of your stakeholding in the issue.

So, for example, the proposition might be for a major fast food chain outlet to be built right next a school—a school that they then would support through generous sponsorship.

On your panel you might have:

- The fast food franchisee
- The principal of the school, excited by the new library that they'll now be able to afford
- The chair of the PTA, concerned about the proximity and associated traffic increases
- An anti-fast-food activist who is appalled by the whole thing
- A politician, excited by the precedent it sets for other education funding opportunities
- The builder who would be completing the project, who is talking up the proposal's value as tackling unemployment in town

That's kindling a-plenty for a spirited debate.

The discussion proper

Each stakeholder would have an opportunity to make a short statement, but the focus of the whole exercise is very much on the questions that follow—from members of the audience, and from fellow panelists.

Moderation is essential

You can't just light this one and stand well back—the moderator will be frenetically busy throughout:

- Choosing who speaks, and in what order
- Ensuring nobody speaks too long, and that there is parity among total speaking times
- Interrupting and insisting on relevance when a question is not really being answered
- Creating questions for the panel when the room seems unable to come up with one otherwise
- Rephrasing questions that are woolly/don't make sense so that

the panelists have something clear to answer (even if the question ends up asking something slightly different)

- Keeping the discussion firing by intelligently creating follow-up questions, and directing them to stakeholders who are likely to react the most strongly.

Whoever is normally running debate training sessions is usually best suited to take this role on, but don't discount the possibility that one of your more capable students could moderate like this.

Shuffle & continue

A variation on this drill is ring a bell after a few minutes, and have everyone swap seats...and personas. So the student being the anti-fast-food activist might suddenly now find they're the franchisee...the students need to continue seamlessly, even though they're now advocating for a completely different position.

Parts of the Speech

THE FOCUS IS STRUCTURE, as several students combine to give a single speech. Each student will have been assigned a different section of the speech, combining into a seamless delivery of the whole. A great way to help students understand speaker roles, and how each speech is built.

26

Good for: Note Taking • Novice Development • Structure & Roles • Working Co-operatively

How this works

This drill is essentially the same as a regular debate, but with one key difference: instead of each speaker on a team giving their own speech in turn, several speakers would *combine* to deliver the speech. Similar to the way dual news anchors take turns to read out an entire story, one speaker would start, another would pick up where they left off, while another would finish.

A transcript of the resulting speech should be unified and seamless enough to read as if it were conceived and delivered by one person—not easy if the eight minutes featured four different people speaking for a couple of minutes each.

Structure, not time

Because the focus is very much on identifying and populating archetypal structural placeholders for each speech, it doesn't make sense to allocate each speaker a set time. Instead, they've got a specific *job* to do; once they've completed their job, the next speaker takes over.

So, for example, a 1st Affirmative with a team of 5 might divide their speech in the following way:

> **Speaker 1:** Introduces the topic, defines the key terms
>
> **Speaker 2:** Outlines the team's case and model
>
> **Speaker 3:** Outlines case division, bulletpoints what 1st and 2nd Aff will each be covering
>
> **Speaker 4:** 1st Aff's argument #1, with supporting evidence
>
> **Speaker 5:** 1st Aff's argument #2, with supporting evidence, closing

This is illustrative only—you can readily repurpose to match however you prefer your own students to structure their debates.

Scripted walkthroughs

If you're working with first time debaters, it's worth actually writing out exactly what each speech segment would say, and have them read it out word-for-word as if lines in a play. This allows them to experience being part of a well-structured debate, without the exercise possibly being derailed by a student being unable to conjure content at the right time—or conjuring content that actually falls entirely outside their brief, thereby further confusing those speakers to follow. You can eventually wean the novices by replacing scripts with bulletpoints, and then their own notes.

Shuffle to master

If you really want students to understand the various structural elements inside each speech–and the order in which they should fall— have them deliver the same speech multiple times, but shuffle which student is responsible for which section each time.

So in our example above, the speaker who originally had to *introduce the topic and define key terms* might be responsible for *outlining the case division and bulletpointing* in the second run-through.

Pass the Parcel

27

THE FAMILIAR BIRTHDAY-PARTY trimmings are reassuringly disarming for apprehensive students: the student must speak on whatever topic is revealed when the music stops and the layer is unwrapped. It's how that parcel is *built* though that makes this game so versatile for debate & speaking coaches.

Good for: Impromptu Speaking · Novice Development · Teambuilding

How this works

Just like its birthday party archetype, the prepared parcel consists of multiple layers of wrapping; it's just that when the parcel stops with a student, instead of unwrapping toys or sweets between layers, the student reveals the topic for a speech that they have to give on the spot.

Color coded difficulty

You can heighten anticipation—and tension—by color coding the layer's wrapping:

If the parcel seems to be **red** at the moment, that might mean that a really tough topic awaits. **Green** might indicate something more friendly.

Blue might be something to do with current affairs. **Orange** could indicate a weird topic inside that will require lateral thinking. **Black** might mean you have to speak super-fast and fit your entire reply into 10 seconds.

Alternatively, the colors might indicate how long the speech must be. A **grey** parcel doing the rounds

might mean someone is about to present a 15 second speech. But if the next layer is **pink**, then that might require 3 minutes.

It's up to you—whatever you decide, the wrapping colors give students a teaser as to what they might be in for, while still retaining mystery and the suspense of a Big Reveal.

More fun if they built it

An engaging option with this game is to allow students to collaborate on building the parcel in the first place, with each student contributing and then wrapping a topic, perhaps as part of a separate session on TOPIC BINGO ▶ 47.

This then means that as each topic is unwrapped during the game, as well as the original revelation of:

Who has to speak on this?

there's now also:

Ok. Which student was responsible for *this* topic?

Great for getting students laughing and getting to know each other

a little better—those playing will usually take great delight if the topic they produced was acclaimed as being challenging/quirky/memorable in some way...and so will work hard in subsequent drills to produce topics that are challenging, quirky and memorable.

Extending this

Remember, the unwrapped layers can reveal whatever you like, which means that you don't have to limit the challenges to being impromptu speeches on a revealed topic. A layer could be a question about something in the news. Or a challenge to say the alphabet, but make it last exactly 60 seconds, without referring to a clock. Or a requirement that the next speech be delivered with hands in pockets and eyes closed.

It's your session. You can randomize whatever you like. The game framework simply ensures that the drills you wanted to do anyway happen with laughter.

💬 Poisoned Words

THERE WILL COME A TIME when every public speaker or advocate has to choose their words very...carefully...but without *sounding* like they're being careful. This drill is all about not being able to say what you really would like to, finding alternatives quickly, and still delivering with fluency and credibility.

28

Good for: Brevity · Impromptu Speaking · Poisoned Words · Speechcraft · Teambuilding

💬 How this works

Every speaker has to accommodate two elements that our outside their control.

The first element is the **topic**, which they must speak to through their 60 second speech.

The second element is a **prohibition**: poisoned word(s) that they're not allowed to use in their speech, but that—given the topic—are words they are highly likely to *want* to include.

Their job is not just to get through the speech without using the poisoned words, but to do so *as naturally and credibly as possible*—if they have to fish for alternatives (and they will!), they have to do so without appearing inconvenienced in the slightest.

💬 Some examples

Let's assume the topic is

"ways to lower the road toll"

The next step is to brainstorm words that would normally appear in a speech that addresses that topic...

so you can then declare those words off-limits.

So for our topic on lowering the road toll, banning any of the following is going to make life tricky for whoever is at the podium:

"Car"
"Accident"
"Deaths"

Getting to the 60 second mark is definitely possible, but doing it without looking like you're carrying a teetering pile of crockery through a ward filled with sleeping new born babies is another matter entirely.

Similarly, if the topic were:

"commercial whaling should be banned"

then some candidates for poison words might be:

"ocean"
"whale"
"Japan"

Of course, some of these poison words would be more difficult to avoid than others. A prohibition that prevents a student from saying "ocean" is going to be challenging;

banning the word "whale" however really does make the speaker's job almost impossible. (You try it...it's not easy).

💬 Alternative poisons

Poisons don't have to be topical words. They can be ordinary words, like "the" or "of"; the aim again is to create a disconnect between what the student would *like* to be able to say, and what they're actually *allowed* to say.

Another option is to ban a letter of the alphabet: the student can say whatever they like, save for words that contain that letter. Not so bad if the letter is "D". Positively brutal if you go for "T" or "E".

And if you really want to test a student? Create a list of several poisons that operate simultaneously. So for the "ways to lower the road toll" topic, the student might not be allowed to say the word "car" or "deaths, or use any two syllable words...good luck ☺

Preassembled Debates

ARMED WITH NOTHING BUT THE ORIGINAL SPEAKING NOTES, can your students recreate a debate they've never seen? And can those in the original source debate create palm cards so clear that such a feat is possible?

29

How this works

This drill is a slightly easier version of EXPERT PRESS CONFERENCES ▶ 33; instead of working just from the adjudicator's notes though, this time they are given speaker's palm cards from an actual debate.

The students won't have seen the notes previously, or the debate itself, and will have limited time to get their head around the content. Their job? To deliver their speech as if they had created these notes themselves, as they play their part in reconstructing the debate itself.

When the debate's over, have the students watch the video of the original debate...how close was their reconstruction? Did they actually manage to do a better job than their source?

Preparing for this

You'll need a video recording of a debate, together with (ideally) the original palm cards—or, if they're not available/legible—then a set you've mocked up.

Because the focus is on students interpreting notes, rather than coming up with content of their own, the palm cards need to list every point made in the debate, together with any supporting examples, and all rebuttals.

Remember: ultimately the students are trying to recreate the original debate, without ever having actually heard it. It's important therefore that the palm cards reflect everything from the original debate, but nothing beyond.

Briefing the students

Tell the students the topic, but remind them that their job is *reconstruction*, not to *win the debate*. This means not augmenting what's in front of them with brilliant new points of their own; it also means not leaving out any listed points, no matter how weak they may believe them to be. The whole palm cards, and nothing but the palm cards.

This means that the students' job is still very much advocacy; not so much for their side of the topic, but for each dot-point in front of them.

The challenge is to be able to sell these points better than the original debaters were able to, irrespective of whether they believe the points to be strong or weak.

The Big Swap

A fun way to create source debates for this drill is to have two different groups conduct and video debates in separate rooms, on different topics.

Once they're done, all the palm cards are collected, and then passed to the other room. Each group then tries to recreate the debate that was just happening next door, armed only with the palm cards they've just been given.

At the conclusion of those attempted recreations, reveal the videos of the originals...again, how close were they? Plenty of scope for conversations about bulletpointing and palm card construction in the aftermath.

Prompt Sheet Speeches

A SINGLE PAGE, PACKED WITH information, trivia, analysis, quotes and memorable facts about a single topic. The student's challenge? Spend just 10 minutes with it, and then give a presentation that has them sounding like an expert.

30

Good for: Examples & Evidence • Impromptu Speaking • Note taking • Speechcraft • Teambuilding

How this works

This drill works best on a conveyer belt: as one student is giving a presentation, the next is backstage with a different information sheet, preparing the presentation to follow. To keep those watching engaged, have them take notes, or assign them elements they need to be giving feedback on (see **MONOTRACK ADJUDICATORS ▶ 23**)

A less confronting option is to hand everyone the same sheet, with the students taking turns giving the same presentation. You can then start with the more confident students, who can provide examples for the less confident/experienced students to model their own presentations on.

Safety net, not crutch

Students are welcome to have the original information sheet in front of them as they present, but shouldn't look like they're depending on it—it's there just in case they get stuck. The more they can memorize in the 10 minutes, the better.

How to create sheets

It doesn't take as long as you might think. Simply choose your topic, then google the stats/info/quotes you need. The more quirky and memorable the information, the easier it will be for the students to give engaging presentations; the more structured and considered it is, the easier it will be for students to present a nuanced argument. It's usually best to make sure both are on the same page; students can then cherry pick whatever suits their preferred presentation style.

So, for example, if the topic was Antarctica, you might seed some interesting trivia:

• Antarctica is the only continent without a time zone. Scientists there either go by the time of their homeland, or that of their supply line of equipment.

• Antarctica is not just the coldest place on earth, but also the driest; it hasn't rained there in more than 2 million years.

• Antarctica is 12 million square miles bigger in winter.

To balance this, you might also seed some more weighty issues; perhaps some information about mining potential, and ways in which nations might try to lay claim to Antarctica's natural resources.

Throw in a couple of quotes as well, and your speakers should have plenty of material to construct their presentation:

"If Antarctica were music it would be Mozart. Art, and it would be Michelangelo. Literature, and it would be Shakespeare. And yet it is something even greater; the only place on earth that is still as it should be. May we never tame it."

Andrew Denton

Fiction as fact

Too serious? Throw in one sheet where all the facts are made up. If the student presents well—and the facts sufficiently plausible—they may just fool everyone.

Quotemaster

31

THE RIGHT QUOTE at a key moment can transform a debate, but getting those stars to align is not always so easy. In this drill, the students are given a proposition to defend or attack, and then race to find the quote that is Just Right from a pool of dozens of candidates...

Good for: Engagement · Quotemaster · Novice Development · Speechcraft · Teambuilding · Working co-operatively

How this works

First you'll need an extensive list of quotes, so that students have plenty to hunt through. Give every group a copy, and a highlighter.

Write a proposition on the board, and the race is underway...which student (or group) can find the quote that is most relevant? First to put their hand up gets to claim whatever quote they read out.

Students need to be careful though: Once they've claimed a quote, they're not allowed to claim another, possibly better option. So they'll have to balance being *fast* with being *considered* and *thorough*.

Scoring

Give points for being the first to find a relevant quote of any sort; give more points to someone who then finds an even better one. Maximum points for the quote you had in mind.

Once all the relevant quotes have been collected, record the scores, write up a new proposition, and move on to round two.

Try one for yourself

"That there are no justifications for breaking the law"

Which of these quotes would be most useful in *opposing* that motion?

A) It is dangerous to be right in matters on which the established authorities are wrong. **Voltaire**

B) It is not what a lawyer tells me I may do; but what humanity, reason, and justice tell me I ought to do. **Edmund Burke**

C) Never think that war, no matter how necessary, nor how justified, is not a crime **Ernest Hemingway**

It's the *process* of selection that is so valuable in this activity—students will have plenty to discuss as they weigh the merits of their shortlisted quotes. Along the way, they'll end up looking at the topic from angles they might never have considered otherwise.

Choosing quotes

There are plenty of quality searchable quote collections online. Here's what to look for: For *beginner students*, ensure the quotes are about a range of clearly differentiated big issues—poverty, war, feminism, social security, patriotism—so that finding the right quote can be as simple as eliminating those that are obviously irrelevant.

For *more experienced debaters*, you can make the hunt much more difficult—and the final selection process more nuanced—by having multiple quotes that all target the same issue, but each with their own subtly different take. The challenge then is not finding a quote that's merely good, or close, but the best possible for the given topic—a process that will generate plenty of discussion within the groups.

Reason Tennis

32

TWO STUDENTS, HEAD TO HEAD, each taking turns to come up with a fresh defense for the given proposition. The first student to hesitate, repeat an existing defense, or come up with something weak/irrelevant loses the point. Using tennis scoring, with a new topic for every point, who will win the game?

Good for: Engagement • Impromptu Speaking • Novice Development • Teambuilding

How this works

Choose your two combatants, issue the statement to be defended, and then flip a coin to see who speaks first. Unlike regular debates, the students won't be arguing with each other, but instead will be taking turns coming up with their own arguments in support of the resolution. Because they're not allowed to reuse any point that's already been made, eventually the well will run dry... the challenge is to make sure that happens to your opponent first.

Scoring

If one of the student *restates* an existing point, shows any sign of *hesitation* when it's their turn, or comes up with something that's not helpful to the proposition because it's *weak* or *irrelevant*, they lose the point.

Following tennis conventions, this would be 15-0, or 0-15, depending on whether the person who conceded the point was the person who started ("served"), or went second ("received"). Just like real tennis, the person serving has an advantage.

Points, not speeches

This game works best if the points are flowing quickly—the students should aim to use as few words as they need to convey their idea, rather than give extended speeches.

The adjudicator is central to keeping this moving: as soon as they understand what the point is well enough to make a quick note, they would simply say "OK". As soon as the other speaker hears that, it's time for them to make a point of their own. (They will need to keep notes too... it can get tricky trying to remember exactly what's been said so far, particularly if you have two good students who are up for a while).

Rhyme ✓; Repeat ✗

Responses are still legal if they *rhyme* with earlier points, as long as they are demonstrably a new point in their own right. So, for example, even if a student had previously highlighted the economic benefits of the proposal, coming up with an entirely different economic benefit could count as a new point—it will be up to the adjudicator to make that determination.

Otherwise though, arguments that are merely differently worded versions of previous points would get buzzed out, as would those that simply explain previously made points in more detail, or reskin old points in fresh examples.

Quantifying hesitation

To defuse any arguments about whether a response was prompt enough, consider using a 3-2-1 countdown before each answer is due. To avoid conceding the point, the next speaker would have to produce their response before the countdown hits zero.

King of the Hill

Another variation is to forget all about tennis scoring, and for the contest to be sudden death—when you're buzzed out, you sit down. The victor stays at the podium, and a fresh challenger takes them on... how many wins in a row can your most capable students produce?

Rebuilding the Debate

33

A TOUGHER VERSION OF **PREASSEMBLED DEBATES ▶29** ; armed just with the adjudicator's flow sheet, can two teams recreate a debate they've never actually seen? Given that they can only include what's listed— and must include *everything* that's listed—how close will they be to the video of the original?

Good for: Rebuttal • Structure & Roles • Working Co-operatively

How this works

Divide the group into two teams, one responsible for preparing the aff, the other the neg. Hand each team plenty of copies of the flow—the idea is for everyone involved to have ready access to it during the discussions that will follow.

The teams then need to use the flow to figure out exactly what each speaker would have said, and then prepare their speeches accordingly.

Not trying to win

The drill is a little like those Civil War battle re-enactments—the aim is to recreate what actually happened, rather than compete. So if the flow indicates that aff loses partly because they fail to counter a key opposition point, then in the debate they must fail to counter that point. If the flow indicates that a neg speaker sits down after only 90 seconds, then 90 seconds it is. And if the flow shows that same speaker wasted most of that time rebutting an insignificant aff factual error, then that's what they must do.

The point is, this is a warts-and-all recreation of the original debate. Even if a speaker thinks up a brilliant, debate-winning rebuttal, unless their corresponding speaker was credited with that rebuttal in the flow, they're not allowed to say it.

It's about the prep

While the exercise culminates in a debate, most of the work is in the discussions beforehand, as each group works with the flow as if it were the cipher to a puzzle. Not everyone involved in helping prepare these debates actually needs to be speaking in the actual debate to benefit, so the groups can be larger than debate-team-sized.

Put the video on

Once the re-enactment is complete, watch the original debate. Students usually surprise themselves with how close they actually were—particularly if the flow was comprehensive and clear—which will leave them with a whole new appreciation of the power of flowing in the first place. (That's the whole point)

No ordinary flow

Most adjudication flows are not made with other readers in mind. The following elements in particular will confuse, and will need to be tidied if students are to have any chance of rebuilding the debate:

- **Illegible handwriting**

- **Inconsistent, arbitrary or unclear symbols**—every symbol in the flow should be clearly explained in a key.

- **Unclear abbreviations.** The adjudicator may well have known that "NGPr" means "Not the Government's Problem", but it's not reasonable to assume that others will have the RAESP* to guess that

If in doubt be available to answer questions before the debate prep starts—students should know exactly what every word, squiggle, line, box and abbreviation means.

*Requisite Acronym Extra Sensory Perception

Rescuing Boring

AS ANY POLITICIAN KNOWS, great manner can make even otherwise questionable material sound oddly compelling. So how engaging can your students be, even when the material is excruciatingly *boring?* They're about to find out....

34

Good for: Impromptu Speaking · Novice Development · Speechcraft · Teambuilding

How this works

Unlike most other speaking drills, the student is not free to come up with their own speech. Instead, you'll be giving them a script, which they must read word-for-word—the only freedom they have is on *how* they deliver it.

To make matters worse, this is not the script of a famous speech, or a compelling argument. It's something dull, long-winded, pointless or repetitive—something that ordinarily no person at a lectern would want to have to read, and no audience would want to have to sit through.

Such as?...

A **page from a phone book** is a great start. You could follow that with **oven cleaner instructions**. If the audience is still awake, then one of those **End User License Agreements** that nobody ever reads, but now one poor student has to read out in full.

In each case, the student's job is to use every trick of speechcraft to bring the texts to life—variation in pacing and intonation, gestures,

dramatic pauses, eye contact that addresses the room as a whole, but then quite suddenly focuses on individuals, as they speak with enthusiasm and engagement that would be more fitting for an opening ceremony, an industry-changing product launch, a State of the Union address, a closing to a jury...

The message to the students? If they can keep an audience engaged with these dull words, what will be possible with words that are *worthy?*

Not mere overacting

The early rounds of this game usually descend into absurdity as the students try to out-melodrama each other. But the aim here is not *hamming it up*, but *persuasion*; they need to be reminded that over-dramatizing their delivery is just as harmful to their ability to persuade as delivering it like Marvin The Depressed Robot.

Instead they should be trying to credibly infuse their speech with one or more of the classic speechcraft delivery elements—it's usually worth stopping the drill for a few minutes

to brainstorm just what these elements are. Their next attempt at the boring text then becomes an etude in these elements.

If they're struggling at all, declare an element that they need to be obsessed with: so the text might still be dull, and they still might not have many ideas for how to rescue it, but they can definitely ensure they *maintain eye contact*, or *vary their intonation* or [insert your preferred speechcraft delivery element here].

If that's a delivery element that the student normally struggles with, so much the better.

Try the reverse

So the students can make *boring text compelling*...could they equally make *compelling text dull?* Similar to the exercise **UNSPEECHES ▶ 48**, their job would be to take one of the great historical speeches, and deliver it in such a way that nobody—*nobody*—would ever have remembered it, had it been said that way.

💬 Side Effects

35

A KEY FACTOR in being able to build a case—or demolish one entirely—is to be able to clearly articulate what *consequences* are likely to flow from the ideas being floated. This drill is all about helping students assess propositions in terms of the flow-on changes they might produce—good or ill, intended or otherwise.

Good for: Novice Development • Rebuttal • Teambuilding • Working Co-operatively

💬 How this works

Give the student a proposition that represents a break from the status quo:

> That schools should only be open at night time

The task then is for them to come up with as many different consequences that policy might produce, were it implemented.

So, for example here, the students might list:

> With schools now closed while parents are working, families would need to find alternative care for their children.

> In promoting a shift to awake-at-night, asleep-during-the-day, we might see a return to vitamin D deficiency diseases such as rickets.

> In promoting a shift to awake-at-night, asleep-during-the-day, we might see a decrease in the incidence of skin cancer.

> Night-only school would require a significant shift in public transport scheduling.

And so on. The students are not trying to construct a case, but instead simply brainstorm as many consequences as possible, no matter how left field.

💬 Choosing propositions

For beginner students, Big Crazy Ideas are going to fire their imaginations most readily:

> That everyone in the world should have to spend a year of their life living in a poverty-stricken country.

> That the Olympic Games should feature sports where the competitors fight to the death.

> That every country in the world should have its own nuclear weapons.

More advanced students can work directly with policy statements, much as they would have to deal with in debates anyway:

> That we should cancel all foreign aid until the budget is in surplus once more.

💬 Fractal side-effects

You can extend this drill by having students examine the consequences of the consequences. So to the proposition for every person in the world to have to spend a year in a poverty-stricken country, students might initially suggest the following consequence:

> **"A surge in international travel, as everyone on the planet who is not already living in a poverty-stricken country is now required to travel at some point"**

The consequence of that consequence might be:

> **"An increase in aircraft-caused carbon emissions"**

These second-degree-of-separation conclusions might occasionally be tenuous, but that's not the point here—it's all about developing the students' "if this, then what might result?" skills, so they can produce such analysis effortlessly and coherently in actual debates.

Someone Else's Notes

I T'S NOT QUITE IMPROMPTU, because the student is speaking from notes...it's just that these notes were written by someone else. Can they pull together a compelling speech from someone else's bullet points?

36

Good for: Impromptu Speaking · Speechcraft · Structure & Roles · Teambuilding

How this works

This drill is in two parts:

1) Students create their notes for a given topic, as if they were about to give the speech themselves. Those notes are then collected, shuffled, and redistributed among all the students, ensuring that no student ends up with their own notes.

2) Armed just with the notes they've now inherited—and without the opportunity to speak to the author for any sort of clarification—each student has a shot at giving the speech.

Place word limits

The easiest way to guarantee accurate delivery of the author's original intentions is for each student to write out every word; to combat this temptation, enforce a strict word limit on the notes themselves. This will ensure that students will use bulletpoints and keywords, rather than full sentences; however the fact that the notes have to be understood by someone else will also force the student to make those keywords and bulletpoints meaningful. If you've ever looked at your own notes mid-speech and wondered what on earth it was talking about—and we've all done it—you'll understand exactly why this is a skill worth developing.

Enforce stick-to-script

To keep the focus on the quality and clarity of the notes themselves—rather than just the ability of a strong impromptu speaker to completely ignore the notes and improvise whatever they like—speakers are constrained by what's in the notes. If a point is not specifically listed, they can't talk about it.

Making it competitive

In this twist, two students will be speaking on each topic, each working from exactly the same notes. One of the students will be the author of those notes, the other simply an inheritor; when the speeches are both done, the audience then needs to vote for who they thought the author actually was.

The challenge here for the inheritor is to see how many audience members they can fool: can they deliver the speech with such continuity and confidence that it sounds as if it was theirs all along?

Of course, every vote they receive is really a win for the author of the notes too—because of the stick-to-script rule, good speeches will really only be possible with good notes.

World's worst notes

While this drill is much easier if the inherited notes are clear and well structured, that's a luxury that's not always available. To help students prepare for reality, issue a set of confusing, hard to read, badly structured notes, and give the student 60 seconds to think...can they get up and give a compelling speech anyway? (How often is the "URGENT" palm card a team mate passes to their 3rd speaker all but indecipherable like this?)

Another variation is to simulate a nightmare that confronts all speakers sooner or later—have them speak *after you've removed a page of notes at random.* (The dreaded missing palm-card scenario!)

◌ Soothsaying

37

ANY TEAM THAT HAS EVER BEEN ambushed by a case they didn't anticipate—or by another team that correctly anticipated what main argument would be used against them—will know the value of being right about the line your opponents end up taking. This drill is all about honing those skills.

Good for: Engagement · Opposition Prep · Rebuttal · Structure & Roles · Working Co-operatively

◌ How this works

In advance of the session, you need to choose a topic, and then come up with what you feel are the strongest 5 points you can for each of both affirmative and negative, just as if you were going to have to present—and defend—both sides for yourself. Then rank those arguments from strongest to weakest, 1-5 for each of aff and neg.

At the session itself, tell the assembled students what you've done, and give them the topic, but don't reveal any of your points, or your ranking.

The groups are then sent away; their time-limited job is to create a ranked list of 10 arguments for each side, with what they feel is the strongest argument at 1, weakest at 10.

Once they're called back, you reveal your list, one item at a time, as they score it against the guesses they had come up with.

◌ Scoring

Teams score points as follows—remember, they will have come up with 10 arguments for each side, while your pre-prepared list will only have come up with 5.
With that in mind:

- If one of their #1 arguments also matched one of your #1 arguments, they score 10 points.

So if they correctly listed both your #1 affirmative and negative arguments as their #1, they'd score 20 points.

- If any of the arguments in their top 5 were in your list, they score 3 points for each.

- Any arguments that were on your list, but that they had ranked in positions 6-10 score 1 point.

◌ Head-to-head

A more challenging way to run the same drill is to have aff and neg compete directly to anticipate each other's points.

To accomplish this, each team would create two lists.
- The "our points" list is the team's own arguments: 6 points that the team would use to support their own position on the topic, whether aff or neg.
- The "their points" list is 6 points they think their opponents will have selected for themselves. When all the arguments for both teams are revealed, the teams compare what they *predicted* against what their opponents *actually selected* for themselves:
Any point your team had that the other team predicted is eliminated.
Any point that the moderator rules is not worthy of the topic is also eliminated. This is to ensure that teams don't list points that cannot be anticipated simply because they're ridiculous (*"School uniforms should be compulsory, because thermonuclear war will rage for 10,000 years otherwise"*)
The team with the most points still standing wins.

Speed Bulletpointing

38

THE STUDENT AT THE PODIUM is given an article, and 60 seconds to turn it into bullet points. When time is up, the article is removed, and—speaking only from the bullet points they just created—he or she must give a 2 minute speech summarizing the article they just read.

Good for: Examples & Evidence • Impromptu Speaking • Note taking • Triaging

This is no drill

The whole exercise is modeled on the sort of **pre-research** debaters have to do as they parse masses of potential source material for prepared topics. No debater will have the time to carefully read every potentially relevant journal feature, news report, opinion piece and webpage—they have to be able to get their head around each candidate source fast, be able to tell immediately whether it's *useful*, and what can be *extracted* from it.

Like everything else debaters do, this takes practice—hence the inclusion of this game.

The cone of silence

A revealing variation on this game is to give several students the same source material, but ensure that they are unable to hear each other's speeches.

What follows will be an honest insight into just what they're taking in, what they're overlooking, and what they were perhaps misunderstanding entirely—four different speakers should end up producing four very different speeches, particularly if the source material was complex.

To make it easier

- Keep the source article short
- Ensure it's clearly structured and easy to scan with subheaders, and (if you really want to help) highlighted passages
- Choose a topic that the student is likely to have some existing knowledge of
- Avoid jargon heavy topics
- Ensure it's well written, preferably with punchy, shorter, easy-to-digest sentences.
- Extend the preparation time
- Allow them to prepare in silence, off stage.

To make it harder

- Make the source article longer
- Ensure it's difficult to scan by ensuring there are no bolds or subheaders, ideally just masses of running text. (One giant paragraph is even tougher)
- Choose a topic that the student is likely to have no idea about
- Lots of jargon
- Look for academic writing, with plenty of passive voice, constant qualifier words and endless nested clauses.
- Shorten the preparation time
- Force them to prepare at the podium, while the rest of the class runs a loud discussion on something different entirely.

Making it *crazy*hard

Give the student no preparation time whatsoever(!) Armed with the article itself—which they're not allowed to read out or quote from in any way—they have to talk *while* they're scanning it. It's the debating equivalent of juggling chainsaws while bungee jumping from a low-orbit spacecraft.

Starter Thoughts

39

THE STUDENTS HEAR THE START of a sentence—something opinionated and considered that was clearly going somewhere. However, just as it's getting interesting, it just stops cold...the student's job is to complete the thought as seamlessly as if it were their own.

Good for: Impromptu Speaking • Novice Development • Teambuilding

How this works

The student at the podium might be given the following thought starter:

> "The greatest challenge facing older people today..."

Their job is then to *restate* the thought-starter, and then *finish the thought*:

> "The greatest challenge facing older people today is that they're likely to live much longer than any generation before them. Combine that with the fact that there are more of them than ever before, and how do we ensure they're supported without bankrupting social security in the process?

You can use the same thought-starter with a different student—they would have to come up with a completely different take:

> "The greatest challenge facing older people today is that they're the last of their kind. Medical advances mean that elderly people in this decade are likely to be the last generation of old people who will actually have to put up with aging."

Finding starters

Simply harvest sentences from articles or interviews, then trim away the second part of each thought.

So an ambassador may have been quoted as saying:

> "Instead of spending so much on defense, nations should be thickening the ties of trade. Peace is purchased, one trade deal at a time."

After pruning, students might be presented with:

> "Instead of spending so much on defense..."

Or you might run with:

> "Peace is purchased..."

Either way, the student has plenty of options. Following a similar process, you'll end up with topics like these:

> "Fame is overrated because..."
> "Science's greatest accomplishment has been..."
> "This country could halve the road toll in 10 years if we would just..."

Easier starters

For less experienced students, you can steer clear of topics that require any sort of complex analysis, and instead look to starters that are rooted in the everyday and familiar:

> "Summer is better than winter because..."
> "School would be more fun if..."
> "If I won $1 million, I would..."

Extending this

If a student is thoroughly comfortable *completing* a thought, see if they can take it the extra step and also *defend* it, as they field questions from the floor. (Similar to the HOSTILE PRESS CONFERENCE ▶ 17 drill)

More challenging still is to require a student to complete the same starter several times in a row—*but to finish it in a completely different way each time.* How many versions can they come up with before they stumble or repeat themselves? (See also GROUNDHOG IMPROMPTUS ▶ 14)

💬 Stat Forger

40

THE STUDENT IS GIVEN A TOPIC to speak on, but instead of supporting their points with research, they must cite statistics that they make up on the spot*. Why would you have students do such a thing? It's all about marking *where* stats should go—placeholders that students can research properly later. *Sudents who do this drill win up to 43.5% more debates.

Good for: Examples & Evidence • Novice Development • Speechcraft • Teambuilding

💬 What this drill is for

There are two keys to using statistics effectively in debates:

- the first is having the right Stat to hand (see STATMASTER ▶ 41), which is an issue of research.

- the second is knowing exactly *when* in the debate stats would have the greatest impact, which is more to do with speechcraft.

This drill is all about isolating and practicing that second skill—instead of stopping everything to research the information they need, students simply make up something that would act as a placeholder. *Here is where my stat would go*, is the message.

💬 How it works

Students are given a proposition which they must speak to, laying out 2-3 points. They must support each point with statistics that confirm the truth and wisdom of their proposal... the twist is that they won't have such statistics to hand, so they're going to Make Them Up.

So, for an affirmative supporting the proposition that education should always be free, they might make the point that putting a price on education deters those who can least afford to pay. Now comes time to back up that assertion...if only there was a stat that demonstrated that very concern.

There might not be just yet, but the whole point of this game is to identify exactly where such a stat ought to go, and then go ahead any make up a placeholder stat so that preparation can keep moving fowards.

It's similar to preparing a speech, and writing "great example goes here" before you acually have created an example of any sort.

💬 What they might say

In our example topic about education being free, the student might say something like this

> "The hard reality of applying a price to education is that you create a barrier to entry. In a recent survey of school leavers in the United States, 62% said that the cost of education was a significant factor in their decision as to which schools they would apply to. Ladies and Gentlemen, that's insane...the only thing that should be keeping you out of whatever school you want to go to is if your marks are too low."

Note the shameless—and entirely fabricated—stat in the middle (that 62% stat is 100% made up).; note too though that it's exactly where the right stat *should* eventually go, which is the drill very much doing its job. All that's needed is to replace the placeholder with a genuine and researched statistic, but that's actually a different phase of preparation.

Of course, what turns up then will likely be different:

> Last year, university admissions boards confirmed a 10% reduction in enrollments, mirroring almost exactly the 12% increase in fees.

It's really not at all the same as the stat the student had guessed, but useful nonetheless. (And, for the purposes of this page, entirely made up. Please don't quote it.)

💬 Statmaster

41

SIMILAR TO QUOTEMASTER ▶ 31, this game is a mad scramble as teams race to claim the stat hidden in the list that would perfectly support—or undermine—the given topic. Designed to give students an appreciation for the power of the well-matched stat...and the tepid impact of stats that are Close But Not Quite What You Need.

Good for: Engagement · Examples & Evidence · Novice Development · Speechcraft · Teambuilding · Working Co-operatively

💬 How this works

First you'll need to have created an extensive list of stats, so that there are plenty for students to have to hunt through. Give every group a copy, and a highlighter.

Write a proposition on the board, and the race is underway...which student (or group) can find the statistic that is most relevant? First to put their hand up gets to claim whatever stat they read out.

Students need to be careful though: Once they've claimed a stat, they're not allowed to claim another, possibly better option. So they'll have to balance being *fast* with being *considered* and *thorough*.

💬 Scoring

Give points for being the first to find a relevant stat of any sort; give more points to someone who then finds an even better one. Maximum points for the stat you had in mind.

Once all the relevant stats have been collected, record the scores, write up a new proposition, and move on to round two.

💬 How to choose stats

There are plenty of quality searchable quote collections online. Here's what to look for:

For **beginner students**, ensure the stats are about a range of clearly differentiated big issues—poverty, war, feminism, gun control, nuclear power—so that finding the right statistic can be as simple as eliminating those that are obviously irrelevant.

For **more experienced debaters**, you can make the hunt much more difficult—and the final selection process more nuanced—by having multiple stats that all target the same issue, but each with their own subtly different focus. The challenge then is not finding a stat that's merely *good*, or *close*, but the *best possible* for the given topic.

Each round will probably take less than a minute for beginner students; advanced students may find themselves puzzling and debating within their own group for much longer before being prepared to push the buzzer.

💬 Try one for yourself

"That we should end the War on Drugs"

Assuming they all come from reputable sources, which of these quotes would be most useful in *supporting* that motion?

A) In 2011, almost half of federal inmates – 48 percent – were in prison for drug crimes.

B) Every day in the US, 2,500 youth (12 to 17) abuse a prescription pain reliever for the first time.

C) Heroin overdoses have caused more deaths than traffic accidents in the past several years.

💬 It's in the seeking

Ostensibly this exercise is about sorting through lists, but what you'll hear when the drill is running is *intense discussion* as the students argue the merits of the possible choices—whether they think they can debate or not, they'll actually be deep in the middle of one.

The Story Chair

THIS DRILL IGNORES all the technicalities of case preparation and rebuttal, and instead focuses on raw public speaking. The challenge? In 2 minutes—and *for* 2 minutes—tell a well known children's story.

42

Good for: Impromptu Speaking · Inner Clock · Novice Development · The Story Chair · Teambuilding

Keeping it friendly
Because the speech will be a retelling of a story the student knows well, content and structure are both taken care of in advance—the content is known to them, and the structure is a linear narrative, starting with "Once Upon a Time."

With *what* they're saying able to run pretty much on autopilot, they're free to focus on *how* they're saying it.

Pacing to 120 seconds
With the entire story needing to last exactly 2 minutes, the student will need frequent time updates to help them pace their progress. If we're at the 90 second mark, and still hearing about how the three bears are thinking of going for a walk in the forest, then the student has some serious compressing to do—just as a 1st Aff speaker would have to if they hear that first bell, and still have two points left to make.

Throwing a curve ball
If you have a confident student who could use the challenge, you can dial up the difficulty by introducing a small variation on the story—this means that they'll still be able to run on autopilot for most of it, but will be responsible for creating a little new content.

> "Up next we have Dashiel, who will be retelling the Three Little Pigs... but at the end of this story, the wolf is going to win."

Note-free zone
Because they're telling a story they already know, there should be no need for palm cards. No matter how nervous a student might be normally about speaking without notes, this is a drill that they should be able to handle without a prompt in sight.

Running it as a team
A variation on this drill is to have half a dozen students at the podium, each contributing a sentence to the story, as they take turns to piece together the entire tale.

It's easier, in that each student has less to contribute; harder in that you have no control over what it is you must segue from. Can produce unexpectedly hilarious results if one of the students starts messing up details of the story.

Candidate stories
One option is classic fairy tales and fables, too many to list here:
- Ugly Duckling
- Snow White and the Seven Dwarfs
- Cinderella
- Little Red Riding Hood
- Sleeping Beauty
- Three Little Pigs
- Hansel and Gretel
- Goldilocks and the Three Bears
- Jack and the Beanstalk
- Tortoise and the Hare

Google *Brothers Grimm, Hans Christian Andersen, Mother Goose* or *Aesop* for plenty more.

Or condense *epic*
If you have a student who thinks they're up to it, forget fairy stories and go novels or movies instead. Harry Potter—in two minutes(!)—your time...starts...now...

Three Columns

43

A RAPID-FIRE GAME THAT REGULARLY calls upon every student in the room, while drilling the basic flow of making an *assertion*, providing a *reason* in support, and then citing *evidence* to support the reason, so the process is second nature when they actually debate.

Good for: Engagement • Examples & Evidence • Impromptu Speaking • Rebuttal • Structure & Roles • Teambuilding

How this works

Divide your students into three lines, have them sit down, except for the first student in each line, who remain standing, ready to go first.

Each of these standing students then makes a different contribution to the same argument. The student at the head of the first line makes a **statement**, the student at the head of the second gives a **reason** in support, while the student at the head of the third line cites **evidence**.

An example

Let's imagine the first speaker makes the following statement:

"That cats are better pets than dogs"

The second speaker might provide the following reason

"Dogs are much more dangerous than cats, making them unsafe for children."

It falls to the third speaker to provide some evidence—or given that there's no time to research, something that sounds like evidence:

"Every year 3,400 children are hospitalized because of dog attacks in the US."

Were this a real debate, the third student would have been able to research the exact stat; their job here is to show that they understand what sort of stat would help the case, so they'd know what to research in the first place.

Rotating the lines

Once the three speakers are done, they move to the back of the *next* line. So the student who just made the statement moves to the back of the reason line; the student who just gave the reason moves to the back of the evidence line, while the evidence student moves to the back of the statement line.

They then gradually work their way to the front of their new queue, at which point their next turn will see them working in a different role from last time.

High turnover

One of the great advantages of this game is that each complete turn usually takes less than 30 seconds, so you'll be able to rotate quickly through all the students present. Even if you're at the back of a queue with 10 people in front of you, you're only 5 minutes from your next turn.

Spoon fed assertions

This drill depends heavily on initial assertions that are fertile with opportunity for those who must justify it—not all students will be equipped to come up with such statements. If your group is inexperienced, you might want to have your first column simply read a prepared assertion they've pulled from a hat.

Extending this drill

One way to take this drill further is to add a fourth column—students in this line would be required to *refute* the initial statement.

Alternatively, you could expect that those in the reason and evidence queues to provide more than one reason, and evidence to match.

🗨 Time Lords

MOST DEBATE AND SPEAKING formats work to time limits, but being able to judge the passage of time while you're at the podium can be maddeningly difficult. This drill has students focusing on exactly that, as they fine tune their inner clock, and learn ways to compress—or stretch—their speech.

44

Good for: Brevity · Engagement · Impromptu Speaking · Inner Clock · Novice Development · Speechcraft · Teambuilding

🗨 How this works

In this drill, it really doesn't matter what the student says, but it does matter how long they say it for.

Start by removing or masking all visible timepieces in the room. The students will then be given:

1) A topic to speak on. Something that the students will have no problem coming up with material for.

2) A time they must speak for. It doesn't have to be conventional debating speech length—better in fact to keep it short, so that there's high turnover of students at the podium. 45 seconds works well.

Each student then has a shot at speaking for as close to that time as they possibly can. As the timekeeper, you won't be ringing bells or giving any sort of hints; simply stop the stopwatch when they stop, and record how close they were.

The only exception to the non-intervention rule would be a ceiling of (say) three times the given time limit, to manage students who genuinely have no idea, and might otherwise bring the whole drill to a crashing halt with a never-ending speech. (There's always one)

🗨 Taking multiple shots

This drill can take a little adjusting to—it's worth allowing students a few shots at the same speech, as they start to develop a feel for just how to pace things to meet the target.

That way even if they're not amongst the Most Accurate students in the room, they can still improve on their own personal bests, while those students who were within a couple of seconds on their first attempt can see if they can hit the center of the target next time.

🗨 Extending the range

How will the students fare if they have to give a speech on the same topic, but now targeting a completely different time? What may have just worked so well for 55 seconds will require a complete rethink for a 90 second version. Or a 12 second version. Or—if you have time—an 8 minute version.

🗨 Charting it

A fun—and illuminating—way to turn all these times into meaningful data is to graph the results as they come in, after which you can discuss any trends that might emerge.

So: when students have to speak for 3 minutes, do they generally *underestimate,* or *overestimate* how long they've been speaking? What happens if the target times are much *shorter?* Much *longer?* If the topic is *more complex?* Or something the speaker *feels passionately about?*

The aim is for students to leave with the understanding that time-skills can be practiced just like any other skill, together with a better understanding as to whether their own clock tends to run slow, or hot.

Time Out Debates

WHAT IF TEAMS WERE ALLOWED TO stop the clock after each speaker, huddle, discuss what they've just heard, and collectively *prepare* their response? Surely the standard of debate would be higher, because less would be missed? Time out debates makes it possible.

45

Good for: Engagement · Examples & Evidence · Note Taking · Opposition Prep · Rebuttal · Reflecting · Structure & Roles · Triaging · Working Co-operatively

How this works

The setup for this drill is as for a standard debate in whatever format you normally use: create your teams, announce the topic, give the sides time to prepare.

There's a key difference in how the debate itself runs: instead of each new speaker immediately following the last, teams have the ability to take "time out" between speeches to confer.

The result is normally a much more thorough and rigorous debate; less is missed, while speakers have invaluable extra time to get their head around their own responses.

Time outs? How long?

There's two ways you can run this. One is to have a set time-out of (say) 5 minutes between every speech. Another more tactically interesting option though is to run it as chess players do, and give each team a total timeout pool for the entire debate that they can then distribute as they wish.

So if that total is 15 minutes, then there's nothing stopping them from using 14 minutes after the very first speech...but that would leave them with only 60 seconds of timeouts for the rest of the debate.

Part of the challenge in the chess-based system is for teams to know when a moment in the debate warrants extra preparation time, and when perhaps they can simply push through.

What is the time for?

The timeouts are designed to give teams a chance to reflect on what they've heard so far:

- Make sure they have all the key opposition points and themes listed, triaged, and rebuttals prepared for the most telling.

- Identify all rebuttals the opposition has used, and prepare counters to them, replacing good rebuttals and examples with great ones.

- Give the next speaker time to think, and go over their own notes.

By the time the speaker stands up, a lot of additional thinking will have gone into their response—hence the tendency for this format to produce higher level debates.

The team is king

The additional emphasis on collaboration during the debate means that non-speaking team members become much more valuable than they normally would be, when their feedback is otherwise limited to mid-speech whispered ideas and scribbled notes. This means that much larger teams than normal are viable—there can be several non-speaking members, all making a difference.

For younger debaters, the format also lends itself to the coach's direct involvement—the coach can be there, leading and moderating these timeout discussions, in much the same way that junior football codes allow their coaches right there on the pitch.

💬 Tongue Twisters

46

A FUN CHANGE-UP for students who have otherwise just been hard at work with something dry. Invite those who think they can tame the tongue-twister to come to the podium. Count how many reps they get through before it all collapses in a flaming wreck. (Oh, it will...)

Good for: Engagement • Novice Development • Speechcraft • Teambuilding

💬 How this works

Write the tongue twister up on the board, give your debaters 20 seconds to practice it. The room will fill with demented chanting and laughter as the first students fall victim to the tongue twister's traps. (Try saying those last three words fast, over and over...)

Then call for volunteers, so that the whole adventure is off to a positive start. Set a ceiling of (say) 10 repetitions, and count as they go. Any slips—and if it even *seems* like a slip, it is—and they're out.

💬 If they get to 10

The battle switches to how fast they can get through 10. Have the students experiment with which syllable transitions they can afford to push, and which still will need care; with focusing on particular syllables; on being aware of where their tongue is, on when they breathe.

And then ask any students who get to 10 reps if they have any tips for how they managed their feat.

💬 Some particularly tricky ones to try *

You'll burn through a lot of tongue twisters in a session—here are some that are sure to test even the most clinically articulate and self-possessed of students.

- Good blood, bad blood
- Top chopstick shops stock top chopsticks
- Toy boat
- Red leather, yellow leather
- Rubber baby buggy bumpers
- Thin chips, thick chips, lick-your-lips chips
- Black bug bit a big black bear
- Pad kid poured curd pulled cold
- Top cop
- Mixed Biscuits
- Rush the washing, Russel
- Unique New York
- An ape hates grape cakes
- Daddy draws doors
- Friendly fleas and fire flies
- Cuthbert's cuff links
- Stupid superstition
- Santa's Short Suit Shrunk
- Eleven benevolent elephants
- Willy's real rear wheel
- Pirates Private Property
- Flash message
- Frogfeet, flippers, swimfins
- Robert Wayne Rutter
- Scissors sizzle, thistles sizzle
- He threw three free throws
- Real rock wall
- She sees cheese
- Mummies make money
- Preshrunk silk shirts
- Crisp crusts crackle and crunch
- Which wristwatches are Swiss wristwatches?

Just try saying that header over and over fast...

💬 Topic Bingo

SECRET TOPICS MIGHT BE *HIDDEN* before a debate, but that doesn't mean they have to be a *surprise*. One of the keys to preparation is knowing what to prepare: this drill is all about students being able to anticipate likely topics for themselves.

47

Good for: Engagement • Working Co-operatively

💬 How this works

First of all, prepare a master list of 50 topics that you feel are likely candidates for inclusion in debate rounds—the topics you choose should represent a broad cross-section of current events, ongoing controversies, and debate chestnuts.

Divide the students into groups and give them half an hour of thinking time; their job is to guess as many of the topics you came up with as possible.

At the end of the half hour, reveal your list one topic at a time, as groups keep tally of just how many they managed to guess correctly.

💬 Scoring

Groups would give themselves 3 points for any topic that is (with slight wording variations, and the fact that the topic may be stated in the negative permitted) exactly what you had, 1 point for a topic that was relevant because it targeted the same broad issue. Students can only score points from each of their listed topics once.

💬 An example

If one of the topics you listed was:

> "That the death penalty should be abolished "

Then if a group had listed

> "That capital punishment should be outlawed"

they would receive the full 3 points, as would a group that listed

> "That capital punishment should be an option for serious violent crimes",

because it's essentially the same topic viewed from the other side. (Most of the research done would be equally useful in both debates).

A candidate for 1 point might be something peripherally relevant, such as:

> "That a state should have the right to protect itself through extra-judicial killings of its enemies."

While a topic such as

> "Crime does not pay"

would not earn any points at all.

💬 Following up

Once the lists have been assembled and checked against the master list, the big question would be "Given these likely topics, what issues should you be reading up on?"

The point you're making is that General Knowledge for debates might indeed be *general*, but it's not *arbitrary*—with limited time available, it makes sense to triage the development of your areas of expertise to align with likely topic areas.

💬 Alternative scoring

Another way to run this drill is not to be trying match a master list, but for teams to be trying to come up with debating topics that the moderator agrees are likely candidates, but that no other group thought of.

Scoring this time would see you scoring 5 points for every debate topic that the moderator agrees is a candidate, but you then lose one point for every other group that also had that topic.

UnSpeeches

WHAT WOULD HAPPEN if students were under instructions to give not the best, but the *worst* possible speech they could? Unspeeches are great fun, but there's a serious intent: students will learn a lot about best practice in speechcraft by immersing themselves in excruciating examples of what *not* to do.

48

Good for: Novice Development • UnSpeeches • Teambuilding

How this works

The student is given a topic to speak on, and a quirk they must adopt that violates one of the core principles of public speaking.

So, for example, they might have to speak while staring at their feet throughout, or using the most complicated words they possibly can for even the simplest of ideas.

Those watching won't have been told what the mannerism is; the audience's job is to identify what instructions the speaker had been given.

Given the way the student at the podium will be hamming it up, that's usually not a problem. The speeches should really only be 60 seconds or so, but most audiences will have the problem figured out before 10 seconds are up.

Quirks? Such as?

A useful pre-exercise is to start the session by brainstorming possibilities—here are the classics that are likely to emerge:

- Speaking too fast/too slowly
- Absence of inflexion
- Overly dramatic
- No hand gestures/over the top hand gestures
- Hand gestures not corresponding to what you're actually saying
- Speaking too quietly/loudly
- Endless rhetorical questions
- Staring at your notes/the floor
- Repeating what is really the same point over and over
- Filled with fillers: ums, ahs
- Maintaining a speaking tempo that is metronomically unchanging.
- Ignoring the topic completely
- No structure/jumping from random point to random point
- Standing completely still and wooden/moving around so much that its distracting
- Getting constantly lost and sorting through what are obviously completely disorganized palm cards
- Losing your train of thought, and starting over rather than pushing on...again and again...
- Filling your speech with pop culture or personal references that the audience is not necessarily going to be able to relate to
- (tough) Filling your speech with clichés/plagiarized lines
- (tougher still) filling your speech with fallacies
- Looking just over the heads of people as you speak/staring at your feet/one person in particular/changing where you're looking chaotically and over rapidly

To follow up

Now that everyone has seen extreme instances of Archetypal Speaking Blunders, the challenge is for students to be able to identify more subtle manifestations of the same issues. Have students speak again without an assigned quirk...and watch closely to see if they have quirks of their own.

Worthy Plans, Evil Plans

A PRELUDE TO POLICY DEBATES: students are given a major social or economic goal, such as "end child poverty"...their challenge is to outline the steps necessary to get there. The twist that makes this drill fun? Some of these goals are, well, not *nice*...

49

Good for: Novice Development • Teambuilding

How this works

This drill depends on having a sizable pool of goals to draw from, some worthy:

> "Cut violent crime"
>
> "Improve national school science results"
>
> "End cruelty to animals"

And some downright Bond-villain deplorable:

> "Send the country broke"
>
> "Destroy the tourism industry"
>
> "Halve national life expectancies"

Once the goal is revealed, the exercise is all about coming up with what policy changes/laws/initiatives might bring that goal about.

An example list

Let's imagine the stated goal was:

> "End the obesity epidemic"

After a quick brainstorm, you might end up with the following on the board:

> "Tax hike on junk food"
>
> "Mandate that all fast food outlets have to be a brisk 20 minute walk from the nearest car park"
>
> "Health insurance premiums to be proportional to a customer's BMI"
>
> "Show all kindergarten students graphic footage of liposuction surgery"

As with all brainstorms, the aim is simply to collect, not to evaluate yet. That comes next, and how you run it depends on the experience levels of your students:

Option 1: Discussion

For less experienced students, a group discussion of the merits of each idea is a non-threatening way for them to engage in debate without even realizing it.

You'll hear plenty of *"yes, but surely..."*, *"the problem with that is..."* *"Maybe if instead..."*, as students pick apart the submissions. Because the atomsphere is informal, they'll feel they're just chatting about the options, but it's going to look and sound a lot like rebuttal-in-development (it is).

Option 2: Speeches

A more formal—and confronting—version of the drill is to call up students to give 2 minute speeches explaining their proposed solution, and then have them defend it against questions from the audience. Once each of the speakers have had a chance to present and defend their own proposal, the group would vote on which idea they believe is most likely to lead to the given outcome.

Why Evil Plans too?

Not trying to create maniacs here: it's just that Evil Plans are a lot more fun, while exercising the same analysis muscles. So while you could have students *ending* an obesity epidemic, it's much more fun for them to come up with ways to *cause* one. Let your dystopian imaginations run riot, enjoy the creativity of what your students come up with.

⊘ You vs The World

50

DEBATING IS SUPPOSED TO BE FAIR. This drill is not. One student is at the podium. Opposing him/her is *every other student in the room,* who are working as a team. Is the speaker capable enough to hold their own...or perhaps even *win...?*

Good for: Engagement • Note Taking • Opposition Prep • Rebuttal • Reflecting • Teambuilding • Working Co-operatively

⊘ How this works

You need to choose your student carefully for this—they will be the "Solo Speaker", taking on the "Rest Of The World" (ie. the rest of the group); it's every bit as unfair as it sounds.

Give that Solo Speaker the topic, and a space where they can prepare an Affirmative case. While that's happening, the Rest Of The World team will be preparing a case to oppose them.

The debate that follows runs much like a regular debate, but with a few key differences:

1) Once the Solo Speaker's speech is complete, they are banished back to their preparation area, while the Rest Of The World (ie. the rest of the class) plans their response, and selects a speaker to give the 1st Neg speech

2) The Solo Speaker returns to the room to hear that 1st Neg speech, and must reply with a 2nd Aff speech of their own. No preparation time for this, save for whatever thinking they can do while 1st Neg is actually talking.

3) Once the Solo Speaker has completed their 2nd Aff speech, again they are banished to a preparation room, so that the Rest Of The World can confer and plan their 2nd Neg speech. A new speaker is selected to give this speech, the Solo Speaker is invited back to hear it...and so the debate continues for as many rounds as you wish.

⊘ Why it's unfair

1) The Solo Speaker only has whatever they themselves can think of, while the Rest of the World is a team of minds. Each of the Rest Of The World's speeches should represent a "best of" the ideas that were canvassed.

2) With so many people taking notes on the Solo Speaker's speeches, it's very unlikely that any of their important points would slip through unnoticed.

Everything should get dealt with; there's nowhere to hide.

3) The audience will consist entirely of members of the Rest Of The World team, and is hardly neutral. If there is any home-ground advantage to be had here, it always resides with the Rest Of The World team.

⊘ Even more unfair...

Still not tough enough for the Solo Speaker? Try these rule modifications:
• The Solo Speaker has to speak without notes, while the Rest Of The World speakers can use whatever notes they need.
• The Solo Speaker could be given a tough proposition to defend—say "That the world is better off with nuclear weapons"
• The Rest Of the World could have access to the internet or other research materials, while the Solo Speaker only has whatever general knowledge they possess.

For more debate training resources online:

www.debate.training

www.ingramcontent.com/pod-product-compliance
Lightning Source LLC
Chambersburg PA
CBHW061048090426
42740CB00002B/81